More
CROCHET
ICONIC WOMEN

Amigurumi Patterns for
15 Incredible Women
Who Changed the World

CARLA MITRANI

BY BUYING THIS BOOK YOU
ARE HELPING TO SUPPORT
THE WONDER FOUNDATION

DAVID & CHARLES

www.davidandcharles.com

CONTENTS

WELCOME!

Hello my friends! I am so happy to see you again in this new celebration of the power of women. I told you in my previous book that one volume was not enough. And certainly a second isn't either. It is such an inspiring ride to decide which women to tribute. And a difficult one too, because we wish we could include so many more! Lists can be tricky. But we believe we bring you here a variety of incredible women: rulers, fighters, scientists and artists. All of them brave, talented and remarkable.

Let's not forget that many of the things that come naturally to us now are the result of the hard work and courageous actions of these women. Of course, they were complex and certainly not perfect, but nevertheless they were able to move mountains, change the mindset of their time and campaign tirelessly for human rights or the protection of our planet. They shaped the world in which we all live today, always believing in themselves and paving the way for future generations.

Crochet Iconic Women has been an incredible success and nothing has made me happier than receiving photos of your makes honouring those amazing individuals and giving them as inspirational gifts to little girls, teachers, sisters, aunts, mothers and daughters. I sincerely hope to achieve the same with this book and that you will add these new tributes to your influential and motivating collection. And, as I always say, dare to tweak the patterns and come up with new icons of your own. They don't necessarily have to be world famous. Most of the time we find pioneers of change in a nearby neighbour, a boss or a best friend.

So, once again, let's grab hooks and yarns and start crocheting!

Carla

TOOLS AND MATERIALS

HOOKS AND YARNS

All the dolls in this book were crocheted using a 2.5mm (US C/2) crochet hook and 8-ply DK weight cotton yarn. I crochet really tightly, which is important so that holes are not created and the fibrefill toy stuffing won't show through the stitches. If you tend to crochet a bit looser, then you should probably choose a smaller hook.

I only use 100% cotton yarns because I like the feel and finish of cotton; it runs smoothly in your hands when working and it will not pill as acrylic or woollen yarns do, which makes these dolls more durable when intended for children. Cotton also builds a sturdier fabric for stuffed dolls, which will not stretch and will hold the stuffing better, without distorting the shapes and volumes of the bodies.

Crochet hooks

Sizes 2.5mm (US C/2) and 2mm (US B/1). The smaller hook is needed to crochet certain accessories such as: Queen Elizabeth I's crown, Wangari Maathai's plant, Josephine Baker's bananas and Mary Shelley's monster.

Cotton yarn

8-ply DK weight 100% soft cotton. I worked with the following yarn by Hobbii:

8/8 Rainbow Cotton

• Fibre: 100% soft cotton
• Ball weight: 50g (1.8oz)
• Length: 75m (82yds)
• Yarn weight: DK (light worsted)

For Queen Elizabeth I's crown, Wangari Maathai's plant, Josephine Baker's bananas and Mary Shelley's monster, I worked with the following yarn, also by Hobbii:

8/4 Rainbow Cotton

• Fibre: 100% soft cotton
• Ball weight: 50g (1.8oz)
• Length: 170m (186yds)
• Yarn weight: Fingering (super fine)

How much yarn is needed?

One of the best things about making the dolls in this book is that none of them uses an entire 50g ball of yarn. In fact, you can use one ball of skin colour to make two dolls. So save all your leftovers and scraps, because they can become skirts, jackets or hats!

OTHER TOOLS AND MATERIALS

Toy safety eyes

Plastic, black, size 8mm (⅓in) for the dolls and 6mm (¼in) for Frankenstein's Monster.

For safety reasons, if you are planning to give the doll to a small child, you should embroider the eyes using black, dark grey or brown yarn instead.

Stuffing

Polyester fibrefill stuffing – you will need to stuff very firmly!

Scissors and seam ripper

Make sure your scissors are sharp. As for the seam ripper, keep it close: sometimes you won't be happy with where you've sewn something and it's fine to remove it and start over!

Stitch markers

When crocheting in a spiral, it's important to mark the beginning of each round with a stitch marker and move this stitch marker up as you work. You can use paper clips, hair clips or safety pins too. Store them together in a small box or tin.

Tapestry/yarn needle

Use this to sew the arms, hair and other accessories to your dolls. Find one with a blunted tip, so it won't split the yarn, wand with an eye big enough to fit your choice of yarn.

Pins

These can be very helpful to hold certain pieces, like hairbuns, while you sew them. Choose those with coloured plastic or beaded heads so they won't slip inside the doll. Ouch!

Wooden chopstick

This is the secret weapon – there is nothing better than a chopstick to evenly spread the stuffing in complicated, hard to reach places!

Tulles, beads, etc.

Some of these dolls need some extra materials, so be sure to read the list carefully before starting.

Craft bag and pencil case

The best thing about crochet is that you can take your current project everywhere! So be ready to pack your hooks, needles and yarns and continue your work in waiting rooms, on public transportation or in parks!

STITCHES

STITCH ABBREVIATIONS

The patterns in this book are written using US crochet terms. These are listed here, along with their UK equivalents (where applicable):

ch = chain stitch

slst = slip stitch

sc = single crochet (UK double crochet)

sc2tog = single crochet 2 stitches together
(UK double crochet 2 stitches together)

hdc = half double crochet (UK half treble crochet)

dc = double crochet (UK treble crochet)

tr = triple crochet (UK double treble crochet)

FLO = front loop only

BLO = back loop only

beg = beginning

rep = repeat

approx = approximately

* = denotes the beginning of a repeat sequence. Repeat the instructions that follow the * as instructed

STITCHES USED

SLIP KNOT

The slip knot is the starting point of the foundation chain and it does not count as a stitch. Make a loop shape with the tail end of the yarn. Insert the hook into it, yarn over hook and draw another loop through it. Pull the yarn tail to tighten the loop around the hook.

CHAIN STITCH (CH)

Start with a slip knot, then yarn over hook and pull through the loop on your hook to create one chain stitch. Repeat this as many times as stated in your pattern.

SLIP STITCH (SLST)

Insert your hook into the stitch, yarn over hook and pull through the stitch and the loop on the hook at the same time.

SINGLE CROCHET (SC)

Insert the hook into the stitch, yarn over hook and pull the yarn back through the stitch. You will now have two loops on the hook. Yarn over again and draw it through both loops at once.

HALF DOUBLE CROCHET (HDC)

Yarn over hook and then insert your hook into the stitch, yarn over hook and pull the yarn through the stitch (you will have three loops on the hook). Yarn over hook and pull through all three loops on the hook in one go.

DOUBLE CROCHET (DC)

Yarn over hook and insert your hook into the stitch, yarn over hook and pull the yarn through the stitch (you will have three loops on the hook). Yarn over hook and pull through the first two loops on the hook in one go (this will leave two loops remaining on the hook). Yarn over hook one last time and pull through the last two remaining loops on the hook.

TRIPLE CROCHET (TR)

Yarn over hook twice and insert your hook into the stitch, yarn over hook and pull the yarn through the stitch (you will have four loops on the hook). Yarn over hook and pull through the first two loops on the hook in one go (this will leave three loops remaining on the hook). Yarn over hook and pull through two loops again (this will leave two loops remaining on the hook). Yarn over hook one last time and pull through the last two remaining loops on the hook.

SINGLE CROCHET 2 STITCHES TOGETHER (SC2TOG)

Working two stitches together creates a decrease of one stitch, and for the dolls in this book the single crochet decrease (sc2tog) is worked as an invisible decrease. *See Techniques: Invisible Single Crochet Decrease* for detailed instructions and photos.

PICOT STITCH (PICOT ST)

Make three chain stitches. Then crochet one sc in the first of those chain stitches (third chain from hook).

BOBBLE STITCH (BOBBLE ST)

This is the stitch I use to create the nose of each doll. The bobble stitch is a cluster of unfinished double crochet stitches worked into one stitch, achieved by leaving the last loop of each double crochet on the hook, to close them all together at the end. Work a bobble stitch by following these step-by-step instructions:

Yarn over hook (**1**) and insert the hook into the stitch. Yarn over hook again and draw the yarn through the stitch. You now have three loops on the hook (**2**). Yarn over hook again and pull it through the first two loops on the hook (**3**). You now have one unfinished double crochet stitch and two loops remain on the hook.

In the same stitch, repeat the previous steps four more times, to create four more unfinished double crochet stitches into that stitch. You must end with six loops on your hook (**4**).

Finally, yarn over hook and draw through all six loops on the hook at once, to create the cluster (**5**).

If, after finishing, you end up with the bump protruding from the wrong side of the fabric (**6**), just push it towards the outside to build the nose (**7**).

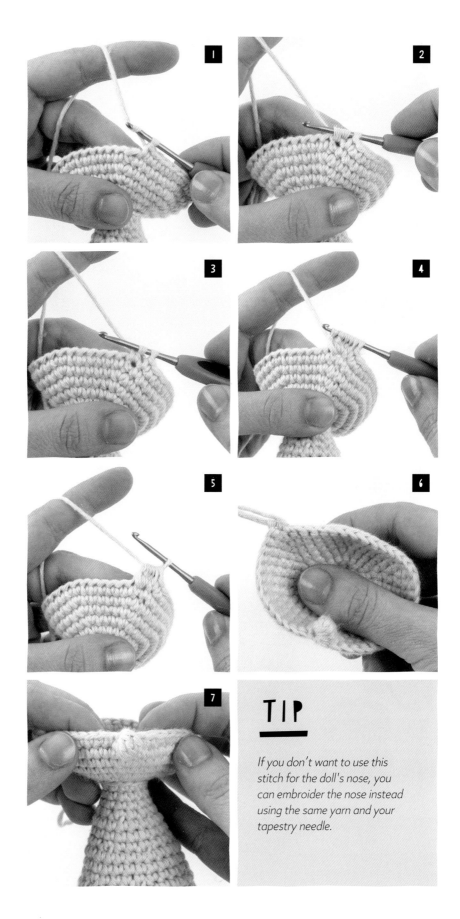

TIP

If you don't want to use this stitch for the doll's nose, you can embroider the nose instead using the same yarn and your tapestry needle.

PROJECTS

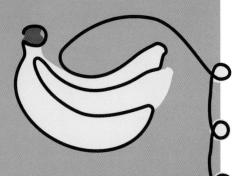

MATERIALS

FOR JOSEPHINE

2.5mm (C/2) crochet hook

100% 8-ply cotton; colours used: skin colour, white, black, yellow, small amount of pink

Yarn needle

8mm (⅓in) safety eyes

Stitch marker

Fibrefill stuffing

White plastic beads

Transparent beading cord

FOR THE BANANAS

2mm (US B/1) crochet hook

100% 4-ply cotton; colours used: yellow

FINISHED SIZE

JOSEPHINE

20cm (7¾in) tall

BANANAS

4cm (1½in) tall

JOSEPHINE BAKER

Why Josephine? Because she wasn't just a showgirl in a banana costume… she was an outspoken activist and even a spy! Born in St Louis, Missouri, in a time of segregation, she pulled herself out of poor origins and devised a vaudeville act full of dance, acrobatics and humour that made her famous in the capital cities of the world! She moved to Paris, where there was no segregation, and in World War II collaborated as a spy with the French resistance, delivering secret messages in invisible ink on music sheets. She so much desired a world where everyone could live in peace, regardless of ethnicity or religion that, to make a point, she adopted 12 children from around the globe, calling her beautiful family her Rainbow Tribe.

LEG 1

Round 1: Using **skin** colour, 6 sc in a magic ring. (6 sts)

Round 2: 2 sc in each st. (12 sts)

Round 3: 1 sc in each st.

Rounds 4 to 8: 1 sc in each st.

Round 9: Change to **white** for the underwear, 1 sc BLO in each st.

Fasten off invisibly (*see Techniques: Fasten Off Invisibly*) and weave in ends (*see Techniques: Weaving In Ends*). Set aside.

LEG 2

Work as for Leg 1, but do not fasten off yarn at the end. We will continue with the body.

BODY

Round 10: Still with leg 2 on your hook, ch 3 and join to leg 1 with a sc (*see Techniques: Joining Legs*), place a stitch marker here for new beg of round, work 11 sc all along leg 1, 1 sc into each ch of 3-ch-loop, 12 sc all along leg 2 and 1 sc into other side of each ch of 3-ch-loop. (30 sts)

Round 11: *4 sc, 2 sc in the next st, rep from * to end. (36 sts)

Rounds 12 to 16: 1 sc in each st.

Stuff the legs firmly at this point.

Round 17: Change to **yellow**, 1 sc BLO in each st.

Round 18: Change to **skin** colour, 1 sc BLO in each st.

Round 19: *4 sc, sc2tog, rep from * to end. (30 sts)

Rounds 20 and 21: 1 sc in each st.

Round 22: *3 sc, sc2tog, rep from * to end. (24 sts)

Rounds 23 to 25: 1 sc in each st.

Start to stuff the body firmly at this point and continue to stuff as you work.

Round 26: *2 sc, sc2tog, rep from * to end. (18 sts)

Rounds 27 and 28: 1 sc in each st.

Round 29: *1 sc, sc2tog, rep from * to end. (12 sts)

Rounds 30 to 32: 1 sc in each st.

Do not fasten off yarn. We will continue with the head.

TIP

Measure the bra strap against the back of your doll and add or subtract one or two chain stitches if necessary.

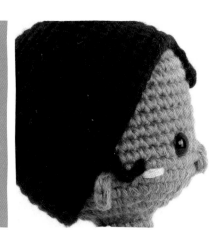

HEAD

Round 33: 2 sc in each st. (24 sts)

Round 34: *3 sc, 2 sc in the next st, rep from * to end. (30 sts)

Stuff the neck area firmly at this point.

Round 35: *4 sc, 2 sc in the next st, rep from * to end. (36 sts)

Round 36: *5 sc, 2 sc in the next st, rep from * to end. (42 sts)

Round 37: 1 sc in each st.

Round 38: 26 sc, 1 bobble st for the nose (*see Stitches: Bobble Stitch*), 1 sc in each st to end.

Be sure to align the nose with the middle of the legs and adjust the positioning if necessary.

Rounds 39 to 47: 1 sc in each st.

Round 48: *5 sc, sc2tog, rep from * to end. (36 sts)

Place safety eyes one round above the nose, with 8 sts between them (*see Techniques: Attaching Eyes*), embroider cheeks with **pink**.

Round 49: *4 sc, sc2tog, rep from * to end. (30 sts)

Start stuffing the head at this point.

Round 50: *3 sc, sc2tog, rep from * to end. (24 sts)

Round 51: *2 sc, sc2tog, rep from * to end. (18 sts)

Stuff firmly.

Round 52: *1 sc, sc2tog, rep from * to end. (12 sts)

Round 53: (Sc2tog) 6 times. (6 sts)

Fasten off and close the remaining stitches through the front loops (*see Techniques: Closing Remaining Stitches Through the Front Loops*). Weave in ends (*see Techniques: Hiding Ends Inside the Doll*).

BRA DISCS (MAKE TWO)

Round 1: Using **yellow**, 6 sc in a magic ring. (6 sts)

Round 2: 2 sc in each st. (12 sts)

Fasten off invisibly, leaving a long tail to sew to the chest.

BRA STRAP

Round 1: Using **yellow** and leaving a long initial tail, ch 18.

Fasten off, leaving a long tail to sew to Josephine's back.

ARMS (MAKE TWO)

Round 1: Using **skin** colour, ch 2, 4 sc in the second ch from hook. (4 sts)

Round 2: 2 sc in each st. (8 sts)

Rounds 3 to 16: 1 sc in each st.

There is no need to stuff the arms.

Round 17: Press the opening with your fingers, aligning 4 sts side by side and sc both sides together by working 1 sc into each pair of sts (*see Techniques: Closing the Arms*).

Fasten off, leaving a long tail to sew to the body.

"All my life, I have maintained that the people of the world can learn to live together in peace if they are not brought up in prejudice."

HAIR

Round 1: Using **black**, 6 sc in a magic ring. (6 sts)

Round 2: 2 sc in each st. (12 sts)

Round 3: *1 sc, 2 sc in the next st; rep from * to end. (18 sts)

Round 4: *2 sc, 2 sc in the next st; rep from * to end. (24 sts)

Round 5: *3 sc, 2 sc in the next st; rep from * to end. (30 sts)

Round 6: *4 sc, 2 sc in the next st; rep from * to end. (36 sts)

Round 7: *5 sc, 2 sc in the next st; rep from * to end. (42 sts)

Round 8: *13 sc, 2 sc in the next st; rep from * to end. (45 sts)

Rounds 9 to 15: 1 sc in each st.

Round 16: 14 sc, ch 8, 1 slst in the second ch from hook and then work 2 slst, 1 sc, 1 hdc, 2 dc. Skip 2 stitches on the edge of the hair piece and crochet 1 sc in the third stitch. Leave the rest of the stitches unworked.

Fasten off, leaving a long tail to sew to the head.

EARS (MAKE TWO)

Round 1: Using **skin** colour, 6 sc in a magic ring. (6 sts)

Close the ring with a slst into the first sc and fasten off, leaving a long tail to sew to the head.

BANANAS (MAKE EIGHTEEN)

IMPORTANT! The bananas are crocheted using the smaller hook size of 2mm (US B/1) and the 4-ply yarn.

Round 1: Using **yellow**, ch 2, 4 sc in the second ch from hook. (4 sts)

Round 2: 1 sc in each st.

Round 3: 2 sc in each st. (8 sts)

Round 4: 1 sc in each st.

Round 5: *1 sc, 2 sc in the next st; rep from * to end. (12 sts)

Rounds 6 to 11: 1 sc in each st.

Stuff firmly.

Round 12: (Sc2tog) twice, 4 sc, (sc2tog) twice. (8 sts)

Round 13: 1 sc in each st.

Round 14: (Sc2tog) 4 times. (4 sts)

Fasten off and close the last round through the front loops. Leave a long tail to sew to Josephine's waist.

ASSEMBLY

Sew the hair to the head (*see Techniques: Sewing the Hair*). When reaching the forehead curl, curve it a bit before sewing it. Make some stitches to close the little gap between the curl and the hair piece (the 2 stitches that you skipped).

Sew the ears to the head. With a bit of **black**, make some stitches to create thin curly sideburns.

Sew the bra discs to Josephine's chest.

Surround Josephine's back with the bra strap and sew it to the discs using both remaining tails, first to the side of one disc and then to the side of the other disc. Using **yellow** and your yarn needle, make a few stitches in between the discs.

Sew the arms to the sides of the body (*see Techniques: Sewing the Arms*).

Sew the bananas to Josephine's waist, to the yellow belt.

Weave in all ends inside the doll.

Thread tiny white beads to the transparent cord to create as many necklaces as you want your Josephine to wear!

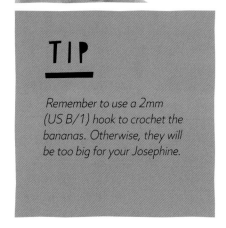

TIP

Remember to use a 2mm (US B/1) hook to crochet the bananas. Otherwise, they will be too big for your Josephine.

"To realize our dreams we must decide to wake up."

MATERIALS

2.5mm (C/2) crochet hook

100% 8-ply cotton; colours used: skin colour, white, black, light grey, dark grey, red, small amount of pink

Yarn needle

8mm (⅓in) safety eyes

Stitch marker

Fibrefill stuffing

FINISHED SIZE

18.5cm (7¼in) tall

ANNE FRANK

Why Anne? Because in a time of darkness, she wrote in her diary about her dreams, hopes and feelings, and without knowing it she produced one of the most powerful and moving pieces of wartime literature, portraying the horrors of Nazism and the Holocaust through the eyes of an innocent girl. Locked up with her family for more than two years in a hidden annex, she never lost hope that things would change, goodness would prevail, and that the world would become a better place. Anne was not given the chance to see it happen, but her diary inspired many generations and was translated to more than 70 languages. Anne's dream of becoming a writer did come true and her spirit lives on in Kitty, her diary.

TIP

When joining the legs, make sure the colour changes in the first leg face you, so they will remain in the back of the doll.

LEG 1

Round 1: Using **black** for the shoes, 6 sc in a magic ring. (6 sts)

Round 2: 2 sc in each st. (12 sts)

Round 3: 1 sc in each st.

Round 4: Change to **white** for the socks, 1 sc BLO in each st.

Rounds 5 and 6: 1 sc in each st.

Round 7: Change to **skin** colour, 1 sc BLO in each st.

Round 8: 1 sc in each st.

Round 9: Change to **white** for the underwear, 1 sc BLO in each st.

Fasten off invisibly (*see Techniques: Fasten Off Invisibly*) and weave in ends (*see Techniques: Weaving In Ends*). Set aside.

LEG 2

Work as for Leg 1, but do not fasten off yarn at the end. We will continue with the body.

BODY

Round 10: Still with leg 2 on your hook, 2 sc, ch 3 and join to leg 1 with a sc (*see Techniques: Joining Legs*), place a stitch marker here for new beg of round, work 11 sc all along leg 1, 1 sc into each ch of 3-ch-loop, 12 sc all along leg 2 and 1 sc into other side of each ch of 3-ch-loop. (30 sts)

Round 11: *4 sc, 2 sc in the next st, rep from * to end. (36 sts)

Rounds 12 to 15: 1 sc in each st.

Stuff the legs firmly at this point.

Round 16: Change to **dark grey** for the skirt, 1 sc in each st.

Round 17: 1 sc BLO in each st.

Round 18: *4 sc, sc2tog, rep from * to end. (30 sts)

Round 19: Change to **light grey** for the shirt, 1 sc BLO in each st.

Round 20: 1 sc in each st.

Round 21: *3 sc, sc2tog, rep from * to end. (24 sts)

Rounds 22 and 23: 1 sc in each st.

Start to stuff the body firmly at this point and continue to stuff as you work.

Round 24: *2 sc, sc2tog, rep from * to end. (18 sts)

Rounds 25 and 26: 1 sc in each st.

Round 27: *1 sc, sc2tog, rep from * to end. (12 sts)

Rounds 28 to 30: 1 sc in each st.

Round 31: Change to **skin** colour, 1 sc BLO in each st.

Do not fasten off yarn. We will continue with the head.

"How wonderful it is that nobody need wait a single moment before starting to improve the world."

HEAD

Round 32: 2 sc in each st. (24 sts)

Round 33: *3 sc, 2 sc in the next st, rep from * to end. (30 sts)

Stuff the neck area firmly at this point.

Round 34: *4 sc, 2 sc in the next st, rep from * to end. (36 sts)

Round 35: *5 sc, 2 sc in the next st, rep from * to end. (42 sts)

Round 36: 1 sc in each st.

Round 37: 26 sc, 1 bobble st for the nose (*see Stitches: Bobble Stitch*), 1 sc in each st to end.

Be sure to align the nose with the middle of the legs and adjust the positioning if necessary.

We will take a break here from the head to work the collar of Anne's shirt. Place a stitch marker in the loop on your hook to secure it and cut the yarn.

COLLAR

For detailed photographs of how to work this collar see *Techniques: Making the Collars*.

Turn the body upside down and join **light grey** in one of the front loops of round 31, at the back of the neck.

Round 1: 1 sc FLO in each st of round 31. (12 sts)

Round 2: 4 sc, (1 hdc, 1 dc) in the next st, (3 dc) in the next st, 1 slst, (1 slst, ch 2, 2 dc) in the next st, (1 dc, 1 hdc) in the next st, 3 sc. (16 sts excluding slst and ch)

Fasten off invisibly and weave in ends.

We will now continue with the head. Rejoin the **skin** colour to where you stopped working the head.

Rounds 38 to 46: 1 sc in each st.

Round 47: *5 sc, sc2tog, rep from * to end. (36 sts)

Place safety eyes one round above the nose, with 8 sts between them (*see Techniques: Attaching Eyes*), embroider cheeks with **pink**.

Round 48: *4 sc, sc2tog, rep from * to end. (30 sts)

Start stuffing the head at this point.

Round 49: *3 sc, sc2tog, rep from * to end. (24 sts)

Round 50: *2 sc, sc2tog, rep from * to end. (18 sts)

Stuff firmly.

Round 51: *1 sc, sc2tog, rep from * to end. (12 sts)

Round 52: (Sc2tog) 6 times. (6 sts)

Fasten off and close the remaining stitches through the front loops (*see Techniques: Closing Remaining Stitches Through the Front Loops*). Weave in ends (*see Techniques: Hiding Ends Inside the Doll*).

SKIRT

Turn the body upside down and join **dark grey** in one of the front loops of round 17, at the back of the body.

Round 1: 1 sc FLO in each st of round 17. (36 sts)

Round 2: *5 sc, 2 sc in the next st, rep from * to end. (42 sts)

Rounds 3 and 4: 1 sc in each st.

Round 5: *6 sc, 2 sc in the next st, rep from * to end. (48 sts)

Rounds 6 to 9: 1 sc in each st.

Fasten off invisibly and weave in ends.

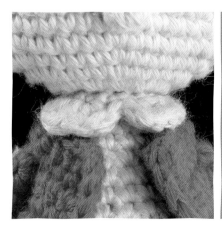

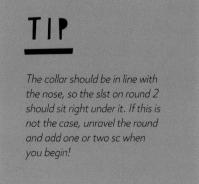

TIP

The collar should be in line with the nose, so the slst on round 2 should sit right under it. If this is not the case, unravel the round and add one or two sc when you begin!

TIP

If you prefer to crochet your Anne without her cardigan, crochet the arms with light grey yarn instead of red.

ARMS (MAKE TWO)

Round 1: Using **skin** colour, ch 2, 4 sc in the second ch from hook. (4 sts)

Round 2: 2 sc in each st. (8 sts)

Rounds 3 to 5: 1 sc in each st.

Round 6: Change to **red** for the cardigan, 1 sc BLO in each st.

Rounds 7 to 17: 1 sc in each st.

There is no need to stuff the arms.

Round 18: Press the opening with your fingers, aligning 4 sts side by side and sc both sides together by working 1 sc into each pair of sts (*see Techniques: Closing the Arms*).

Fasten off, leaving a long tail to sew to the body.

CARDIGAN

The cardigan is actually a vest, but when you put it on your Anne, together with the arms, it will look like a cardigan. The vest is worked in rows from the top down, using **red**.

Row 1: Ch 21, 1 sc in the second ch from hook, 1 sc in each ch to end, ch 1, turn. (20 sts)

Row 2: 4 sc, *ch 6, skip the following 4 sts (to create armhole), 4 sc, rep from * once more, ch 1, turn.

Row 3: 4 sc, *6 sc in the 6-ch-loop, 4 sc, rep from * once more, ch 1, turn. (24 sts)

Rows 4 to 11: 1 sc in each st, ch 1, turn.

Row 12: 1 sc in each st, ch 1, rotate the work 90 degrees clockwise and work 12 sc along the side of the vest, working in the spaces between rows. When you reach the top edge, crochet 20 sc in the remaining loops of the foundation chain. Then ch 1, rotate the piece 90 degrees clockwise again and work 12 sc along the other side of the vest, working in the spaces between rows (*see Techniques: Edging of Flat Pieces*).

Fasten off invisibly and weave in ends.

"In the long run, the sharpest weapon of all is a kind and gentle spirit."

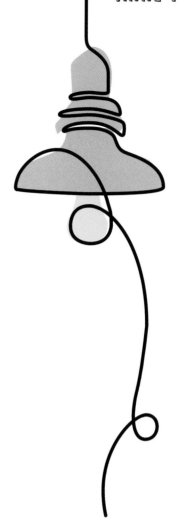

HAIR

Round 1: Using **black**, 6 sc in a magic ring. (6 sts)

Round 2: 2 sc in each st. (12 sts)

Round 3: *1 sc, 2 sc in the next st; rep from * to end. (18 sts)

Round 4: *2 sc, 2 sc in the next st; rep from * to end. (24 sts)

Round 5: *3 sc, 2 sc in the next st; rep from * to end. (30 sts)

Round 6: *4 sc, 2 sc in the next st; rep from * to end. (36 sts)

Round 7: *5 sc, 2 sc in the next st; rep from * to end. (42 sts)

Round 8: *13 sc, 2 sc in the next st; rep from * to end. (45 sts)

Rounds 9 to 15: 1 sc in each st.

Round 16: *1 slst, ch 26, 1 sc in second ch from hook, 1 sc in each st along ch (25 sts); rep from * once more, 2 slst, 1 sc, 1 hdc, 3 dc, 1 hdc, 1 sc, 2 slst, **ch 13, 1 sc in the second ch from hook, 1 sc in each st along ch (12 sts), 1 slst, rep from ** to last st. (18 hair curls)

Fasten off, leaving a long tail to sew to the head.

ASSEMBLY

Sew the hair to the head (*see Techniques: Sewing the Hair*), with the two long hair locks to the left of her forehead (with the doll looking at you). Then part the long locks to the left and secure them with a few stitches to the side. Using a bit of **red**, make 3 or 4 backstitches with your yarn needle to create the 'hair clip'.

Sew the arms to the sides of the body (*see Techniques: Sewing the Arms*).

Slip the vest onto Anne's arms. It will look like a cardigan.

Weave in all ends inside the doll.

TIP

Anne's short hair locks should curl naturally. If they don't, you can help them into shape with your fingers by twirling them.

MATERIALS

FOR WANGARI

2.5mm (C/2) crochet hook

100% 8-ply cotton; colours
used: skin colour, white,
black, petrol blue, light
green, egg yolk yellow,
small amount of pink

Yarn needle

8mm (⅓in) safety eyes

Stitch marker

Fibrefill stuffing

FOR THE PLANT

2mm (US B/1) crochet hook

100% 4-ply cotton;
colours used: light grey,
dark brown and green

FINISHED SIZE

WANGARI

20cm (7¾in) tall

PLANT

8cm (3in) tall

WANGARI MAATHAI

Why Wangari? Because with a very simple idea – teaching the women in her natal Kenya to plant trees to render the land fertile again – she created a ripple effect known as the Green Belt Movement, which expanded to many other countries. More than 50 million trees have been planted in Kenya, empowering communities, and specially women, to protect the environment while helping them earn money. She believed that people's inherent goodness was essential to making change. Wangari went on to become a member of the Kenyan Parliament, advocating for the rights of women, universal education and a more democratic Kenya. In 2004 she was awarded the Nobel Peace Prize, becoming the first African woman to win it.

LEG 1

Round 1: Using **skin** colour, 6 sc in a magic ring. (6 sts)

Round 2: 2 sc in each st. (12 sts)

Round 3: 1 sc in each st.

Rounds 4 to 8: 1 sc in each st.

Round 9: Change to **white** for the underwear, 1 sc BLO in each st.

Fasten off invisibly (*see Techniques: Fasten Off Invisibly*) and weave in ends (*see Techniques: Weaving In End*s). Set aside.

LEG 2

Work as for Leg 1, but do not fasten off yarn at the end. We will continue with the body.

BODY

Round 10: Still with leg 2 on your hook, ch 3 and join to leg 1 with a sc (*see Techniques: Joining Legs*), place a stitch marker here for new beg of round, work 11 sc all along leg 1, 1 sc into each ch of 3-ch-loop, 12 sc all along leg 2 and 1 sc into other side of each ch of 3-ch-loop. (30 sts)

Round 11: *4 sc, 2 sc in the next st, rep from * to end. (36 sts)

Rounds 12 to 16: 1 sc in each st.

Stuff the legs firmly at this point.

Round 17: *4 sc, sc2tog, rep from * to end. (30 sts)

Round 18: Change to **skin** colour, 1 sc BLO in each st.

Rounds 19 and 20: 1 sc in each st.

Round 21: *3 sc, sc2tog, rep from * to end. (24 sts)

Rounds 22 and 23: 1 sc in each st.

Start to stuff the body firmly at this point and continue to stuff as you work.

Round 24: *2 sc, sc2tog, rep from * to end. (18 sts)

Round 25: Change to **petrol blue** for dress, 1 sc in each st.

Round 26: 1 sc BLO in each st.

Round 27: Change to **skin** colour, 1 sc BLO in each st.

Round 28: *1 sc, sc2tog, rep from * to end. (12 sts)

Rounds 29 to 32: 1 sc in each st.

Do not fasten off yarn. We will continue with the head.

HEAD

Round 33: 2 sc in each st. (24 sts)

Round 34: *3 sc, 2 sc in the next st, rep from * to end. (30 sts)

Stuff the neck area firmly at this point.

Round 35: *4 sc, 2 sc in the next st, rep from * to end. (36 sts)

Round 36: *5 sc, 2 sc in the next st, rep from * to end. (42 sts)

Round 37: 1 sc in each st.

Round 38: 27 sc, 1 bobble st for the nose (*see Stitches: Bobble Stitch*), 1 sc in each st to end.

Be sure to align the nose with the middle of the legs and adjust the positioning if necessary.

Rounds 39 to 47: 1 sc in each st.

Round 48: *5 sc, sc2tog, rep from * to end. (36 sts)

Place safety eyes one round above the nose, with 8 sts between them (*see Techniques: Attaching Eyes*), embroider cheeks with **pink**.

Round 49: *4 sc, sc2tog, rep from * to end. (30 sts)

Start stuffing the head at this point.

Round 50: *3 sc, sc2tog, rep from * to end. (24 sts)

Round 51: *2 sc, sc2tog, rep from * to end. (18 sts)

Stuff firmly.

Round 52: *1 sc, sc2tog, rep from * to end. (12 sts)

Round 53: (Sc2tog) 6 times. (6 sts)

Fasten off and close the remaining stitches through the front loops (*see Techniques: Closing Remaining Stitches Through the Front Loops*). Weave in ends (*see Techniques: Hiding Ends Inside the Doll*).

ARMS (MAKE TWO)

Round 1: Using **skin** colour, ch 2, 4 sc in the second ch from hook. (4 sts)

Round 2: 2 sc in each st. (8 sts)

Rounds 3 to 16: 1 sc in each st.

There is no need to stuff the arms.

Round 17: Press the opening with your fingers, aligning 4 sts side by side and sc both sides together by working 1 sc into each pair of sts (*see Techniques: Closing the Arms*).

Fasten off, leaving a long tail to sew to the body.

"When we plant trees, we plant the seeds of peace and hope."

DRESS

Turn the body upside down and join **petrol blue** in one of the front loops of round 26, at the back of the body.

Round 1: 1 sc FLO in each st of round 26. (18 sts)

Round 2: *2 sc, 2 sc in the next st, rep from * to end. (24 sts)

Round 3: 1 sc in each st.

Round 4: *3 sc, 2 sc in the next st, rep from * to end. (30 sts)

Rounds 5 to 7: 1 sc in each st.

Round 8: *4 sc, 2 sc in the next st, rep from * to end. (36 sts)

Rounds 9 and 10: 1 sc in each st.

Round 11: *5 sc, 2 sc in the next st, rep from * to end. (42 sts)

Rounds 12 and 13: 1 sc in each st.

Round 14: *6 sc, 2 sc in the next st, rep from * to end. (48 sts)

Rounds 15 to 18: 1 sc in each st.

Round 19: *7 sc, 2 sc in the next st, rep from * to end. (54 sts)

Round 20: 1 sc in each st.

Round 21: Change to **light green**, 1 sc in each st.

Round 22: Change back to **petrol blue**, 1 sc in each st.

Round 23: Change to **egg yolk yellow**, 1 sc in each st.

Round 24: Change back to **petrol blue**, 1 sc in each st.

Round 25: Change to **light green**, 1 sc in each st.

Round 26: 1 sc in each st.

Fasten off invisibly and weave in ends.

IMPORTANT! Sew the arms to the body now, between rounds 28 and 29 of the body (*see Techniques: Sewing the Arms*).

RUFFLE OF THE DRESS

Turn the body upside down and join **petrol blue** in one of the front loops of round 27, right in the middle of the back of the body.

Round 1: 1 sc in the front loop in the middle of the back (place a stitch marker on the first sc to mark beg of round) and 1 sc in the front loop next to that one, towards the arm. Ch 12. Surround the arm with this chain and insert your hook into the closest front loop on round 27 on the chest of the doll and crochet 1 sc (I left 3 front loops free under the arm). Now crochet 1 sc in each of the following 7 front loops along round 27. This should get you close to the other arm. Once again ch 12, surround the arm with the chain and insert your hook in the closest front loop on round 27 on the back side of the body (once again, I've left 3 free front loops under the arm) and crochet 1 sc in the last two remaining front loops of round 27.

Round 2: 2 sc, 1 sc in each of the 12 chain stitches of the first chain, 8 sc, 1 sc in each of the 12 chain stitches of the second chain, 2 sc. (36 sts)

Round 3: 1 sc in each st.

Round 4: *8 sc, 2 sc in the next st, rep from * to end. (40 sts)

Round 5: Change to **light green**, 1 sc in each st.

Round 6: 1 sc in each st.

Fasten off invisibly and weave in ends.

TIP

You could replace Wangari's crocheted head scarf with one made of a very colourful fabric instead!

HAIR

Round 1: Using **black**, 6 sc in a magic ring. (6 sts)

Round 2: 2 sc in each st. (12 sts)

Round 3: *1 sc, 2 sc in the next st; rep from * to end. (18 sts)

Round 4: *2 sc, 2 sc in the next st; rep from * to end. (24 sts)

Round 5: *3 sc, 2 sc in the next st; rep from * to end. (30 sts)

Round 6: *4 sc, 2 sc in the next st; rep from * to end. (36 sts)

Round 7: *5 sc, 2 sc in the next st; rep from * to end. (42 sts)

Round 8: *13 sc, 2 sc in the next st; rep from * to end. (45 sts)

Rounds 9 to 16: 1 sc in each st.

Fasten off, leaving a long tail to sew to the head.

HEAD SCARF

The scarf is worked in rows, using **petrol blue**.

Row 1: Ch 81, 1 sc in the second ch from hook, 1 sc in each ch to end, ch 1, turn. (80 sts)

Rows 2 and 3: 1 sc BLO in each st, ch 1, turn.

Row 4: 1 sc BLO in each st.

Fasten off and weave in ends.

"No matter how dark the cloud, there is always a thin, silver lining, and that is what we must look for."

LITTLE TREE

IMPORTANT! The tree is crocheted using the smaller hook size of 2mm (US B/1) and the 4-ply yarn.

THE SOIL

Round 1: Using **dark brown**, 6 sc in a magic ring. (6 sts)

Round 2: 2 sc in each st. (12 sts)

Round 3: *1 sc, 2 sc in the next st; rep from * to end. (18 sts)

Round 4: *2 sc, 2 sc in the next st; rep from * to end. (24 sts)

Fasten off invisibly and weave in ends.

THE POT

Round 1: Using **light grey**, 6 sc in a magic ring. (6 sts)

Round 2: 2 sc in each st. (12 sts)

Round 3: *1 sc, 2 sc in the next st; rep from * to end. (18 sts)

Round 4: 1 sc BLO in each st.

Rounds 5 and 6: 1 sc in each st.

Round 7: *8 sc, 2 sc in the next st; rep from * once more. (20 sts)

Round 8: 1 sc in each st.

Round 9: *9 sc, 2 sc in the next st; rep from * once more. (22 sts)

Round 10: 1 sc in each st.

Round 11: *10 sc, 2 sc in the next st; rep from * once more. (24 sts)

Stuff firmly. Take the soil piece and place it over the opening of the pot.

Round 12: 1 sc joining one st of the opening of the pot with one st of the soil, rep from * to the end.

Before fully closing the opening, check if you need to add more stuffing.

Fasten off invisibly and weave in ends.

TREE TRUNK

Round 1: Using **dark brown**, ch 2, 4 sc in the second ch from hook. (4 sts)

Round 2: 2 sc in each st. (8 sts)

Rounds 3 to 8: 1 sc in each st.

Fasten off, leaving a long tail to sew to the soil.

LEAVES (MAKE THREE)

Round 1: Using **green**, ch 11, 1 slst in the second ch from hook, 2 sc, 3 hdc, 2 sc, 1 slst, 3 slst in the last st of the chain (this will allow you to turn and work on the other side of the chain), 1 slst, 2 sc, 3 hdc, 2 sc, 1 slst.

Close with a slst in the first stitch. Fasten off, leaving a long tail to sew to the tip of the trunk.

ASSEMBLY

Sew the hair to the head (*see Techniques: Sewing the Hair*).

Knot the scarf around the head.

Stuff the tree trunk slightly and sew it to the soil. Sew the three leaves to the tip of the trunk.

Using **egg yolk yellow**, embroider little dots to the skirt of Wangari's dress.

Weave in all ends inside the doll.

MATERIALS

2.5mm (C/2) crochet hook

100% 8-ply cotton; colours used: skin colour, dark grey, light grey, light brown, small amount of pink and of red

Yarn needle

8mm (⅓in) safety eyes

Stitch marker

Fibrefill stuffing

FINISHED SIZE

19cm (7½in) tall

JOAN OF ARC

Why Joan? Because she is an icon of courage and audacity. At about the age of 17, she led the French army to victory against England in Orléans, making possible the crowning of the Dauphin as King Charles VII and boosting French morale during the final stages of the Hundred Years' War. When captured by the English she faced trial with bravery and never renounced her faith and beliefs, not even when found guilty of heresy and burnt at the stake. The verdict was later nullified and she was exonerated. Joan was a martyr, a leader and a fighter. Nearly 500 years after her death the Catholic Church made her a saint and she is now one of the patron saints of France, teaching the world that the relentless courage of one person can make a huge change.

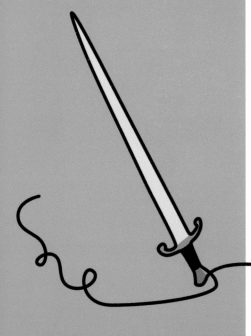

LEG 1

Round 1: Using **dark grey** for the boots, 6 sc in a magic ring. (6 sts)

Round 2: 2 sc in each st. (12 sts)

Rounds 3 to 8: 1 sc in each st.

Round 9: Change to **light grey** for the armour, 1 sc BLO in each st.

Fasten off invisibly (*see Techniques: Fasten Off Invisibly*) and weave in ends (*see Techniques: Weaving In Ends*). Set aside.

LEG 2

Work as for Leg 1, but do not fasten off yarn at the end. We will continue with the body.

BODY

Round 10: Still with leg 2 on your hook, ch 3 and join to leg 1 with a sc (*see Techniques: Joining Legs*), place a stitch marker here for new beg of round, work 11 sc all along leg 1, 1 sc into each ch of 3-ch-loop, 12 sc all along leg 2 and 1 sc into other side of each ch of 3-ch-loop. (30 sts)

Round 11: *4 sc, 2 sc in the next st, rep from * to end. (36 sts)

Rounds 12 to 16: 1 sc in each st.

Stuff the legs firmly at this point.

Round 17: *4 sc, sc2tog, rep from * to end. (30 sts)

Round 18: Change to **dark grey**, 1 sc in each st.

Round 19: Change back to **light grey**, 1 sc BLO in each st.

Round 20: *3 sc, sc2tog, rep from * to end. (24 sts)

Round 21: Change to **dark grey**, 1 sc in each st.

Rounds 22 and 23: 1 sc in each st.

Start to stuff the body firmly at this point and continue to stuff as you work.

Round 24: *2 sc, sc2tog, rep from * to end. (18 sts)

Rounds 25 and 26: 1 sc in each st.

Round 27: *1 sc, sc2tog, rep from * to end. (12 sts)

Rounds 28 and 29: 1 sc in each st.

Round 30: Change to **light grey**, 1 sc BLO in each st.

Round 31: 1 sc in each st.

Do not fasten off yarn. We will continue with the head.

"One life is all we have and we live it as we believe in living it."

HEAD

Round 32: Change to **skin** colour, 1 sc BLO in each st.

Round 33: 2 sc in each st. (24 sts)

Round 34: *3 sc, 2 sc in the next st, rep from * to end. (30 sts)

Stuff the neck area firmly at this point.

Round 35: *4 sc, 2 sc in the next st, rep from * to end. (36 sts)

Round 36: *5 sc, 2 sc in the next st, rep from * to end. (42 sts)

Round 37: 1 sc in each st.

Round 38: 29 sc, 1 bobble st for the nose (*see Stitches: Bobble Stitch*), 1 sc in each st to end.

Be sure to align the nose with the middle of the legs and adjust the positioning if necessary.

We will now start crocheting the collar of Joan's armour, as it will be easier to do so without the finished head. Place a stitch marker in the loop on your hook to secure it and cut the yarn.

COLLAR OF THE ARMOUR

Turn the body upside down and join **dark grey** in one of the front loops of round 30, at the back of the neck.

Round 1: *1 sc FLO, 2 sc FLO in the next st, rep from * to end. (18 sts)

Round 2: *2 sc, 2 sc in the next st, rep from * to end. (24 sts)

Rounds 3 and 4: 1 sc in each st.

Fasten off invisibly and weave in ends.

We will now continue with the head. Rejoin the **skin** colour to where you stopped working the head.

Rounds 39 to 47: 1 sc in each st.

Round 48: *5 sc, sc2tog, rep from * to end. (36 sts)

Place safety eyes one round above the nose, with 8 sts between them (*see Techniques: Attaching Eyes*), embroider cheeks with **pink**.

Round 49: *4 sc, sc2tog, rep from * to end. (30 sts)

Start stuffing the head at this point.

Round 50: *3 sc, sc2tog, rep from * to end. (24 sts)

Round 51: Change to **light brown** for the hair, *2 sc, sc2tog, rep from * to end. (18 sts)

Stuff firmly.

Round 52: *1 sc, sc2tog, rep from * to end. (12 sts)

Round 53: (Sc2tog) 6 times. (6 sts)

Fasten off and close the remaining stitches through the front loops (*see Techniques: Closing Remaining Stitches Through the Front Loops*). Weave in ends (*see Techniques: Hiding Ends Inside the Doll*).

WAIST PROTECTION

Turn the body upside down and join **dark grey** in one of the front loops of round 19, at the back of the body.

Round 1: 1 sc FLO in each st of round 19. (30 sts)

Round 2: *4 sc, 2 sc in the next st, rep from * to end. (36 sts)

Round 3: 1 sc in each st.

Round 4: *5 sc, 2 sc in the next st, rep from * to end. (42 sts)

Round 5: 1 sc in each st.

Fasten off invisibly and weave in ends.

ARMS (MAKE TWO)

Round 1: Using **dark grey** for the gloves, ch 2, 4 sc in the second ch from hook. (4 sts)

Round 2: 2 sc in each st. (8 sts)

Rounds 3 to 10: 1 sc in each st.

Round 11: Change to **light grey**, 1 sc BLO in each st.

Rounds 12 to 17: 1 sc in each st.

There is no need to stuff the arms.

Round 18: Press the opening with your fingers, aligning 4 sts side by side and sc both sides together by working 1 sc into each pair of sts (*see Techniques: Closing the Arms*).

Fasten off, leaving a long tail to sew to the body.

TIP

It is hard to close the hair completely. This is why we crocheted the last rounds of Joan's head using the brown yarn.

HAIR

The hair is worked in rows using **light brown.**

Row 1: Ch 21, 1 slst in the second ch and 1 slst in each the following 4 ch, 1 sc in each ch to end (20 sts = 5 slst + 15 sc), ch 1, turn.

Row 2: 15 sc BLO, 5 slst BLO, ch 1, turn.

Row 3: 5 slst BLO, 15 sc BLO, ch 1, turn.

Rows 4 to 26: Repeat rows 2 and 3 eleven more times, then row 2 once.

Row 27: 5 slst BLO, 8 sc BLO, ch 1, turn.

Row 28: 8 sc BLO, 5 slst BLO, ch 1, turn.

Rows 29 to 48: Repeat rows 27 and 28 ten more times.

Row 49: Ch 1 and bring row 1 and row 48 together, aligning the stitches of both rows. Crochet 1 sc across each pair of stitches, joining one stitch from row 48 with one loop of the foundation chain in row 1.

Fasten off and weave in ends. Turn the piece inside out. Thread your yarn needle with **light brown** and pass it through the stitches of the top opening of the hair. Pull gently but tightly. You can run the needle through the stitches a second time to close the hole a bit more. It won't close completely, but never mind: this is why we crocheted the last rounds of the head in **light brown.**

ASSEMBLY

Sew the hair onto the head (*see Techniques: Sewing the Hair*).

Lift the collar of the armour and sew the arms to the sides of the body (*see Techniques: Sewing the Arms*).

Using **red**, embroider a tiny fleur-de-lis on Joan's chest.

Weave in all ends inside the doll.

TIP

Don't forget to turn the hair piece inside out after crocheting both the ends together.

"To sacrifice what you are and to live without belief is a fate more terrible than dying."

MATERIALS

2.5mm (C/2) crochet hook

100% 8-ply cotton;
colours used: skin colour,
white, denim blue, pink,
fuchsia, light yellow, small
amount of light grey

Yarn needle

8mm (⅓in) safety eyes

Stitch marker

Fibrefill stuffing

FINISHED SIZE

21cm (8¼in) tall

DOLLY PARTON

Why Dolly? Because she is a living legend across generations and music genres. Ever a fighter for what is right and fair, she was one of the first to demand equal payment for women. Larger-than-life, she was never afraid to make fun of herself, her looks and struggles during her career. And instead of hiding those difficulties, she put them forward to inspire others to not be afraid to try and stand under the spotlight. She has composed more than 3000 songs, reaching the Top 10 several times. But her talents don't end there – Dolly became an actress and a very successful businesswoman, opening her own record label and theme park! She shares her success with others through her many charitable organizations.

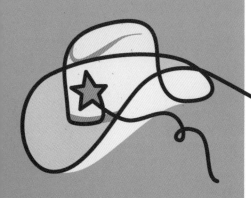

LEG 1

Round 1: Using **white** for the boots, 6 sc in a magic ring. (6 sts)

Round 2: 2 sc in each st. (12 sts)

Rounds 3 to 6: 1 sc in each st.

Round 7: Change to **denim blue** for the pants, 1 sc BLO in each st.

Rounds 8 and 9: 1 sc in each st.

Fasten off invisibly (*see Techniques: Fasten Off Invisibly*) and weave in ends (*see Techniques: Weaving In Ends*). Set aside.

LEG 2

Work as for Leg 1, but do not fasten off yarn at the end. We will continue with the body.

BODY

Round 10: Still with leg 2 on your hook, ch 3 and join to leg 1 with a sc (*see Techniques: Joining Legs*), place a stitch marker here for new beg of round, work 11 sc all along leg 1, 1 sc into each ch of 3-ch-loop, 12 sc all along leg 2 and 1 sc into other side of each ch of 3-ch-loop. (30 sts)

Round 11: *4 sc, 2 sc in the next st, rep from * to end. (36 sts)

Rounds 12 to 15: 1 sc in each st.

Stuff the legs firmly at this point.

Round 16: Change to **white** for the belt, 1 sc BLO in each st.

Round 17: *4 sc, sc2tog, rep from * to end. (30 sts)

Round 18: Change to **pink** for the shirt, 1 sc BLO in each st.

Rounds 19 and 20: 1 sc in each st.

Round 21: *3 sc, sc2tog, rep from * to end. (24 sts)

Rounds 22 and 23: 1 sc in each st.

Start to stuff the body firmly at this point and continue to stuff as you work.

Round 24: *2 sc, sc2tog, rep from * to end. (18 sts)

Rounds 25 and 26: 1 sc in each st.

Round 27: *1 sc, sc2tog, rep from * to end. (12 sts)

Now we will do several colour changes. Remember to join the yarn of the required colour in the last step of the previous st to the change.

Round 28: 7 sc, change to **skin** colour, 1 sc, change back to **pink**, 4 sc.

Round 29: 6 sc, change to **skin** colour, 3 sc, change back to **pink**, 3 sc.

Round 30: 5 sc, change to **skin** colour, 5 sc, change back to **pink**, 2 sc.

Round 31: 4 sc, change to **skin** colour, 7 sc, change back to **pink**, 1 sc.

You should have a skin colour triangle at the front centre of the doll.

Do not fasten off yarn. We will continue with the head.

"The way I see it, if you want the rainbow, you got to put up with the rain."

HEAD

Round 32: Change to **skin** colour, 1 sc BLO in each of the first 4 sts (those in **pink**), 1 sc through both loops in each of the following 7 sts (those in **skin** colour), 1 sc BLO in the last st (in **pink**). (12 sts)

Round 33: 2 sc in each st. (24 sts)

Round 34: *3 sc, 2 sc in the next st, rep from * to end. (30 sts)

Stuff the neck area firmly at this point.

Round 35: *4 sc, 2 sc in the next st, rep from * to end. (36 sts)

Round 36: *5 sc, 2 sc in the next st, rep from * to end. (42 sts)

Round 37: 1 sc in each st.

Round 38: 29 sc, 1 bobble st for the nose (*see Stitches: Bobble Stitch*), 1 sc in each st to end.

Be sure to align the nose with the middle of the legs, and the skin colour triangle at the neck, and adjust the positioning if necessary.

Rounds 39 to 47: 1 sc in each st.

Round 48: *5 sc, sc2tog, rep from * to end. (36 sts)

Place safety eyes one round above the nose, with 8 sts between them (*see Techniques: Attaching Eyes*), embroider cheeks with **pink**.

Round 49: *4 sc, sc2tog, rep from * to end. (30 sts)

Start stuffing the head at this point.

Round 50: *3 sc, sc2tog, rep from * to end. (24 sts)

Round 51: *2 sc, sc2tog, rep from * to end. (18 sts)

Stuff firmly.

Round 52: *1 sc, sc2tog, rep from * to end. (12 sts)

Round 53: (Sc2tog) 6 times. (6 sts)

Fasten off and close the remaining stitches through the front loops (*see Techniques: Closing Remaining Stitches Through the Front Loops*). Weave in ends (*see Techniques: Hiding Ends Inside the Doll*).

ARMS (MAKE TWO)

Round 1: Using **skin** colour, ch 2, 4 sc in the second ch from hook. (4 sts)

Round 2: 2 sc in each st. (8 sts)

Rounds 3 to 5: 1 sc in each st.

Round 6: Change to **fuchsia** for the jacket, 1 sc BLO in each st.

Rounds 7 to 17: 1 sc in each st.

There is no need to stuff the arms.

Round 18: Press the opening with your fingers, aligning 4 sts side by side and sc both sides together by working 1 sc into each pair of sts (*see Techniques: Closing the Arms*).

Fasten off, leaving a long tail to sew to the body.

TIP

Feel free to sew silver sequins or stars to Dolly's outfits. She loves glitter!

TIP

You can knot little pieces of yarn to the bottom end of the jacket to create a fringe.

JACKET

The jacket is actually a vest, but when you put it on your Dolly, together with the arms, it will look like a jacket. The vest is worked in rows from the top down, using **fuchsia**.

Row 1: Ch 21, 1 sc in the second ch from hook, 1 sc in each ch to end, ch 1, turn. (20 sts)

Row 2: 4 sc, *ch 6, skip the following 4 sts (to create armhole), 4 sc, rep from * once more, ch 1, turn.

Row 3: 4 sc, *6 sc in the 6-ch-loop, 4 sc, rep from * once more, ch 1, turn. (24 sts)

Rows 4 to 12: 1 sc in each st, ch 1, turn.

Row 13: 1 sc in each st, ch 1, rotate the work 90 degrees clockwise and work 13 sc along the side of the vest, working in the spaces between rows. When you reach the top edge, crochet 20 sc in the remaining loops of the foundation chain. Then ch 1, rotate the piece 90 degrees clockwise again and work 13 sc along the other side of the vest, working in the spaces between rows (*see Techniques: Edging of Flat Pieces*).

Fasten off invisibly and weave in ends.

HAIR

Round 1: Using **light yellow**, 6 sc in a magic ring. (6 sts)

Round 2: 2 sc in each st. (12 sts)

Round 3: *1 sc, 2 sc in the next st, rep from * to end. (18 sts)

Round 4: *2 sc, 2 sc in the next st, rep from * to end. (24 sts)

Round 5: *3 sc, 2 sc in the next st, rep from * to end. (30 sts)

Round 6: *4 sc, 2 sc in the next st, rep from * to end. (36 sts)

Round 7: *5 sc, 2 sc in the next st, rep from * to end. (42 sts)

Round 8: *13 sc, 2 sc in the next st, rep from * to end. (45 sts)

Rounds 9 to 15: 1 sc in each st.

Round 16: * Ch 9, 1 sc in second ch from hook, 1 sc in each st along ch (8 sts), 2 sc, rep from * to create 13 short hair locks. Then ** ch 21, 1 sc in second ch from hook, 1 sc in each st along ch (20 sts), 1 sc, rep from ** to create 9 long hair locks (*see Techniques: Crocheting Curls*).

Fasten off, leaving a long tail to sew to the head.

COWBOY HAT

Round 1: Using **white**, 6 sc in a magic ring. (6 sts)

Round 2: 2 sc in each st. (12 sts)

Round 3: *1 sc, 2 sc in the next st, rep from * to end. (18 sts)

Round 4: *2 sc, 2 sc in the next st, rep from * to end. (24 sts)

Round 5: *3 sc, 2 sc in the next st, rep from * to end. (30 sts)

Round 6: *4 sc, 2 sc in the next st, rep from * to end. (36 sts)

Round 7: *5 sc, 2 sc in the next st, rep from * to end. (42 sts)

Rounds 8 to 12: 1 sc in each st.

Round 13: *6 sc, 2 sc in the next st, rep from * to end. (48 sts)

Rounds 14 and 15: 1 sc in each st.

Round 16: Change to **pink** for the band, 1 sc BLO in each st.

Round 17: 1 sc in each st.

Round 18: Change back to **white**, 1 sc BLO in each st.

Round 19: *1 sc, 2 sc in the next st, rep from * to end. (72 sts)

Round 20: 1 sc in each st.

Round 21: *2 sc, 2 sc in the next st, rep from * to end. (96 sts)

Round 22: 1 sc in each st.

Round 23: 1 slst in each st.

Fasten off invisibly and weave in ends.

ASSEMBLY

Sew the hair to the head (*see Techniques: Sewing the Hair*) and, with the doll facing you, part 5 of the short locks on her forehead to the left and the rest to the right.

Using **pink**, embroider two straight lines on the skin colour triangle in the neck to mark the edges of the shirt.

Sew the arms to the sides of the body (*see Techniques: Sewing the Arms*).

Slip the vest onto Dolly's arms. It will look like a jacket.

Using **light grey**, embroider the buckle on her white belt.

Shape the crown of the cowboy hat, creating the centre crease and the two dents. Secure the sides of the brim with a few loose stitches.

Place the hat on Dolly's head.

Weave in all ends inside the doll.

"If you don't like the road you're walking, start paving another one."

MATERIALS

FOR QUEEN ELIZABETH I

2.5mm (C/2) crochet hook

100% 8-ply cotton;
colours used: skin colour,
white, light blue, dark grey,
dark blue, burnt orange,
small amount of pink

Yarn needle

8mm (⅓in) safety eyes

Stitch marker

Fibrefill stuffing

5mm (¼in) plastic
pearl beads

Transparent beading cord

FOR THE CROWN

2mm (US B/1) crochet hook

100% 4-ply cotton; colours
used: sunny yellow

FINISHED SIZE

QUEEN ELIZABETH I
21cm (8¼in) tall

QUEEN ELIZABETH I

Why Queen Elizabeth I? Because she ruled England, Ireland and Wales for 44 years all alone and her reign gave birth to a long period of prosperity, known as the Golden Age. Enduring pressure from all sides she avoided marriage, convinced she had the will and power to lead her kingdom herself—no husband needed, thank you! Conspiracies were planned against her, but she frustrated them all. She was intelligent, fierce and courageous. Under her rule English ships sailed the oceans, discovering new trade routes and connecting with the world. During her time literature also flourished, especially English drama, with playwrights like William Shakespeare and Christopher Marlowe producing works we still enjoy today.

LEG 1

Round 1: Using **skin** colour, 6 sc in a magic ring. (6 sts)

Round 2: 2 sc in each st. (12 sts)

Rounds 3 to 8: 1 sc in each st.

Round 9: Change to **white** for the underwear, 1 sc BLO in each st.

Fasten off invisibly (*see Techniques: Fasten Off Invisibly*) and weave in ends (*see Techniques: Weaving In Ends*). Set aside.

LEG 2

Work as for Leg 1, but do not fasten off yarn at the end. We will continue with the body.

BODY

Round 10: Still with leg 2 on your hook, ch 3 and join to leg 1 with a sc (*see Techniques: Joining Legs*), place a stitch marker here for new beg of round, work 11 sc all along leg 1, 1 sc into each ch of 3-ch-loop, 12 sc all along leg 2 and 1 sc into other side of each ch of 3-ch-loop. (30 sts)

Round 11: *4 sc, 2 sc in the next st, rep from * to end. (36 sts)

Rounds 12 to 16: 1 sc in each st.

Stuff the legs firmly at this point.

Round 17: *4 sc, sc2tog, rep from * to end. (30 sts)

Round 18: Change to **light blue** for the skirt, 1 sc in each st.

Round 19: Change to **dark grey** for the belt, 1 sc BLO in each st.

Round 20: *3 sc, sc2tog, rep from * to end. (24 sts)

Now we will do several colour changes. Remember to join the yarn of the required colour in the last step of the previous st to the change.

Round 21: Change to **dark blue**, 10 sc BLO, change to **white**, 4 sc BLO, change back to **dark blue**, 10 sc BLO.

Round 22: 10 sc, change to **white**, 5 sc, change back to **dark blue**, 9 sc.

Round 23: 9 sc, change to **white**, 7 sc, change back to **dark blue**, 8 sc.

Start to stuff the body firmly at this point and continue to stuff as you work.

Round 24: *2 sc, sc2tog, rep from * once more, 1 sc, change to **white**, 1 sc, sc2tog, 2 sc, sc2tog, 1 sc, change back to **dark blue**, 1 sc, sc2tog, 2 sc, sc2tog. (18 sts)

Round 25: 6 sc, change to **white**, 8 sc, change back to **dark blue**, 4 sc.

Round 26: 6 sc, change to **white**, 8 sc, change back to **dark blue**, 4 sc.

Round 27: Change to **skin** colour, 1 sc BLO in each st.

Round 28: *1 sc, sc2tog, rep from * to end. (12 sts)

Rounds 29 to 31: 1 sc in each st.

Do not fasten off yarn. We will continue with the head.

HEAD

Round 32: 2 sc in each st. (24 sts)

Round 33: *3 sc, 2 sc in the next st, rep from * to end. (30 sts)

Stuff the neck area firmly at this point.

Round 34: *4 sc, 2 sc in the next st, rep from * to end. (36 sts)

Round 35: *5 sc, 2 sc in the next st, rep from * to end. (42 sts)

Round 36: 1 sc in each st.

Round 37: 26 sc, 1 bobble st for the nose (*see Stitches: Bobble Stitch*), 1 sc in each st to end.

Be sure to align the nose with the middle of the legs and adjust the positioning if necessary.

Rounds 38 to 46: 1 sc in each st.

Round 47: *5 sc, sc2tog, rep from * to end. (36 sts)

Place safety eyes one round above the nose, with 8 sts between them (*see Techniques: Attaching Eyes*), embroider cheeks with **pink**.

Round 48: *4 sc, sc2tog, rep from * to end. (30 sts)

Start stuffing the head at this point.

Round 49: *3 sc, sc2tog, rep from * to end. (24 sts)

Round 50: *2 sc, sc2tog, rep from * to end. (18 sts)

Stuff firmly.

Round 51: *1 sc, sc2tog, rep from * to end. (12 sts)

Round 52: (Sc2tog) 6 times. (6 sts)

Fasten off and close the remaining stitches through the front loops (*see Techniques: Closing Remaining Stitches Through the Front Loops*). Weave in ends (*see Techniques: Hiding Ends Inside the Doll*).

SKIRT

Turn the body upside down and join **light blue** in one of the front loops of round 19, at the back of the body.

Round 1: 1 sc FLO in each st of round 19. (30 sts)

Round 2: *4 sc, 2 sc in the next st, rep from * to end. (36 sts)

Round 3: 1 sc in each st.

Round 4: *5 sc, 2 sc in the next st, rep from * to end. (42 sts)

Rounds 5 to 7: 1 sc in each st.

Round 8: *6 sc, 2 sc in the next st, rep from * to end. (48 sts)

Rounds 9 to 11: 1 sc in each st.

Round 12: *7 sc, 2 sc in the next st, rep from * to end. (54 sts)

Rounds 13 to 15: 1 sc in each st.

Round 16: 4 sc, 2 sc in the next st, *8 sc, 2 sc in the next st, rep from * 4 more times, 4 sc. (60 sts)

Rounds 17 to 19: 1 sc in each st.

Fasten off invisibly and weave in ends.

HIP PADS (MAKE TWO)

Round 1: Using **dark blue**, 6 sc in a magic ring. (6 sts)

Round 2: 2 sc in each st. (12 sts)

Rounds 3 and 4: 1 sc in each st.

Round 5: *1 sc, 2 sc in the next st; rep from * to end. (18 sts)

Rounds 6 and 7: 1 sc in each st.

Round 8: *2 sc, 2 sc in the next st; rep from * to end. (24 sts)

Rounds 9 to 14: 1 sc in each st.

Round 15: Press the opening with your fingers, aligning 12 sts side by side and sc both sides together by working 1 sc into each pair of sts.

Fasten off, leaving a long tail to sew to Queen Elizabeth's waist.

"I know I have but the body of a weak and feeble woman, but I have the heart and stomach of a king."

TIP

The skirt must hide the Queen's legs. Crochet an extra round or two if necessary.

TIP

Do not stuff the hip pads. Flatten them with your fingers and curve them so they surround the waist.

HAIR

Round 1: Using **burnt orange**, 6 sc in a magic ring.

Round 2: 2 sc in each st. (12 sts)

Round 3: *1 sc, 2 sc in the next st; rep from * to end. (18 sts)

Round 4: *2 sc, 2 sc in the next st; rep from * to end. (24 sts)

Round 5: *3 sc, 2 sc in the next st; rep from * to end. (30 sts)

Round 6: *4 sc, 2 sc in the next st; rep from * to end. (36 sts)

Round 7: *5 sc, 2 sc in the next st; rep from * to end. (42 sts)

Round 8: *13 sc, 2 sc in the next st; rep from * to end. (45 sts)

Rounds 9 to 15: 1 sc in each st.

Round 16: 1 slst, 1 sc, 1 hdc, 10 dc, 1 hdc, 1 sc, 1 slst, 1 sc, 1 hdc, 10 dc, 1 hdc, 1 sc, 1 slst. Leave the rest of the stitches unworked.

Fasten off, leaving a long tail to sew to the head.

HAIRBUNS (MAKE TWO)

Round 1: Using **burnt orange**, 6 sc in a magic ring.

Round 2: 2 sc in each st. (12 sts)

Round 3: *1 sc BLO, 2 sc BLO in the next st; rep from * to end. (18 sts)

Round 4: *2 sc, 2 sc in the next st; rep from * to end. (24 sts)

Round 5: *3 sc BLO, 2 sc BLO in the next st; rep from * to end. (30 sts)

Round 6: *4 sc, 2 sc in the next st; rep from * to end. (36 sts)

Round 7: 1 sc BLO in each st.

Round 8: 1 sc in each st.

Round 9: 1 sc BLO in each st.

Fasten off, leaving a long tail to sew to the head.

CURLY HAIR FOR THE HAIRBUNS

If you look at the hairbuns you've just finished, you'll see the spiral of front loops from the magic ring at the beginning, right up to the last round. We are going to work the curly hair into these front loops.

Join the **burnt orange** in the first front loop around the magic ring: *1 sc in next front loop, ch 3, skip next front loop, 1 sc in the following front loop, rep from * in a spiral to the last 2 front loops on round 9. Leave these unworked.

Fasten off and weave in ends.

HALO

The halo is worked in rows using **white**.

Row 1: Leaving a long initial tail, ch 14, 1 hdc in the third ch from hook, 3 hdc, 4 sc, 4 slst, ch 1, turn. (12 sts).

Row 2: 4 slst BLO, 4 sc BLO, 4 hdc BLO, ch 1, turn.

Row 3: Ch 1, 4 hdc BLO, 4 sc BLO, 4 slst BLO, ch 1, turn.

Rows 4 to 23: Repeat rows 2 and 3 ten more times.

Fasten off, leaving a long tail to sew to the Queen's back.

ARMS (MAKE TWO)

Round 1: Using **skin** colour, ch 2, 4 sc in the second ch from hook. (4 sts)

Round 2: 2 sc in each st. (8 sts)

Rounds 3 to 5: 1 sc in each st.

Round 6: Change to **light blue**, 1 sc BLO in each st.

Rounds 7 to 17: 1 sc in each st.

There is no need to stuff the arms.

Round 18: Press the opening with your fingers, aligning 4 sts side by side and sc both sides together by working 1 sc into each pair of sts (*see Techniques: Closing the Arms*).

Fasten off, leaving a long tail to sew to the body.

CROWN

IMPORTANT! The crown is crocheted using the smaller hook size of 2mm (US B/1) and the 4-ply yarn.

Round 1: Using **sunny yellow**, ch 25, 1 sc in the first chain (the 25th chain from hook) to form a ring, 1 sc in each st along ch. (25 sts)

Round 2: *3 sc, sc2tog, rep from * to end. (20 sts)

Round 3: *3 slst, (2 hdc, picot (*see Stitches: Picot Stitch*), 1 hdc) in the next st, rep from * to end, 1 slst in the first st of the round to finish.

Fasten off leaving a long tail to sew to Queen Elizabeth's hair.

ASSEMBLY

Sew the hair to the head (*see Techniques: Sewing the Hair*).

Stuff the hairbuns and sew them to the sides of the hair.

Sew the crown between the hairbuns.

Sew some pearls between the curls of the hairbuns.

Sew the halo to the sides of the corset, using the two remaining long tails and secure it at the back of the doll with a few stitches.

Sew the arms to the sides of the body (*see Techniques: Sewing the Arms*).

Sew the hip pads to the waist.

Using the **sunny yellow** you used for the crown, embroider little golden dots to the hip pads and laces to the corset.

Make a small necklace with the remaining pearls and the beading cord.

Weave in all ends inside the doll.

TIP

Remember to change your hook for the 2mm (US B/1) one to crochet the crown!

ELLA FITZGERALD

Why Ella? Because she is considered to be the Queen of Jazz, the First Lady of Song, and a cultural ambassador. She pulled herself out of the streets, where she was living as a teenager, to become world famous. The first African-American woman to win a Grammy, she won a total of 13 during her career. She recorded more than 2000 songs and was given the Presidential Medal of Freedom. With her generosity and uniquely uplifting singing style, so understandable, Lady Ella paved the way for other African-American performers. In her late years, when she could perform no more, she founded a charity to help children in need, remembering her own very tough and humble origins.

LEG 1

Round 1: Using **skin** colour, 6 sc in a magic ring. (6 sts)

Round 2: 2 sc in each st. (12 sts)

Rounds 3 to 8: 1 sc in each st.

Round 9: Change to **white** for the underwear, 1 sc BLO in each st.

Fasten off invisibly (*see Techniques: Fasten Off Invisibly*) and weave in ends (*see Techniques: Weaving In Ends*). Set aside.

LEG 2

Work as for Leg 1, but do not fasten off yarn at the end. We will continue with the body.

BODY

Round 10: Still with leg 2 on your hook, ch 3 and join to leg 1 with a sc (*see Techniques: Joining Legs*), place a stitch marker here for new beg of round, work 11 sc all along leg 1, 1 sc into each ch of 3-ch-loop, 12 sc all along leg 2 and 1 sc into other side of each ch of 3-ch-loop. (30 sts)

Round 11: *4 sc, 2 sc in the next st, rep from * to end. (36 sts)

Rounds 12 to 16: 1 sc in each st.

Stuff the legs firmly at this point.

Round 17: *4 sc, sc2tog, rep from * to end. (30 sts)

Round 18: Change to **dark blue** for the dress, 1 sc in each st.

Round 19: 1 sc BLO in each st.

Round 20: *3 sc, sc2tog, rep from * to end. (24 sts)

Rounds 21 to 23: 1 sc in each st.

Start to stuff the body firmly at this point and continue to stuff as you work.

Round 24: *2 sc, sc2tog, rep from * to end. (18 sts)

Rounds 25 and 26: 1 sc in each st.

Round 27: *1 sc, sc2tog, rep from * to end. (12 sts)

Now we will do several colour changes. Remember to join the yarn of the required colour in the last step of the previous st to the change.

Round 28: 7 sc, change to **skin** colour, 1 sc, change back to **dark blue**, 4 sc.

Round 29: 6 sc, change to **skin** colour, 3 sc, change back to **dark blue**, 3 sc.

Round 30: 5 sc, change to **skin** colour, 5 sc, change back to **dark blue**, 2 sc.

Round 31: 4 sc, change to **skin** colour, 7 sc, change back to **dark blue**, 1 sc.

You should have a skin colour triangle at the front centre of the doll.

Do not fasten off yarn. We will continue with the head.

"It isn't where you came from, it's where you're going that counts."

HEAD

Round 32: Change to **skin** colour, 1 sc BLO in each of the first 4 sts (those in **dark blue**), 1 sc through both loops in each of the following 7 sts (those in **skin** colour), 1 sc BLO in the last st (in **dark blue**). (12 sts)

Round 33: 2 sc in each st. (24 sts)

Round 34: *3 sc, 2 sc in the next st, rep from * to end. (30 sts) Stuff the neck area firmly at this point.

Round 35: *4 sc, 2 sc in the next st, rep from * to end. (36 sts)

Round 36: *5 sc, 2 sc in the next st, rep from * to end. (42 sts)

Round 37: 1 sc in each st.

Round 38: 29 sc, 1 bobble st for the nose (*see Stitches: Bobble Stitch*), 1 sc in each st to end.

Be sure to align the nose with the middle of the legs, and the skin colour triangle at the neck, and adjust the positioning if necessary.

Rounds 39 to 47: 1 sc in each st.

Round 48: *5 sc, sc2tog, rep from * to end. (36 sts)

Place safety eyes one round above the nose, with 8 sts between them (*see Techniques: Attaching Eyes*), embroider cheeks with **pink**.

Round 49: *4 sc, sc2tog, rep from * to end. (30 sts)

Start stuffing the head at this point.

Round 50: *3 sc, sc2tog, rep from * to end. (24 sts)

Round 51: *2 sc, sc2tog, rep from * to end. (18 sts)

Stuff firmly.

Round 52: *1 sc, sc2tog, rep from * to end. (12 sts)

Round 53: (Sc2tog) 6 times. (6 sts)

Fasten off and close the remaining stitches through the front loops (*see Techniques: Closing Remaining Stitches Through the Front Loops*). Weave in ends (*see Techniques: Hiding Ends Inside the Doll*).

SKIRT

Turn the body upside down and join **dark blue** in one of the front loops of round 19, at the back of the body.

Round 1: 1 sc FLO in each st of round 19. (30 sts)

Round 2: *4 sc, 2 sc in the next st, rep from * to end. (36 sts)

Round 3: 1 sc in each st.

Round 4: *5 sc, 2 sc in the next st, rep from * to end. (42 sts)

Rounds 5 to 7: 1 sc in each st.

Round 8: *6 sc, 2 sc in the next st, rep from * to end. (48 sts)

Rounds 9 to 14: 1 sc in each st.

Round 15: *7 sc, 2 sc in the next st, rep from * to end. (54 sts)

Rounds 16 to 19: 1 sc in each st.

Fasten off invisibly and weave in ends.

If you want, you could embroider on sequins of the same colour as Ella's dress to make it super shiny!

ARMS (MAKE TWO)

Round 1: Using **skin** colour, ch 2, 4 sc in the second ch from hook. (4 sts)

Round 2: 2 sc in each st. (8 sts)

Rounds 3 to 10: 1 sc in each st.

Round 11: Change to **dark blue** for the dress, 1 sc BLO in each st.

Rounds 12 to 17: 1 sc in each st.

There is no need to stuff the arms.

Round 18: Press the opening with your fingers, aligning 4 sts side by side and sc both sides together by working 1 sc into each pair of sts (*see Techniques: Closing the Arms*).

Fasten off, leaving a long tail to sew to the body.

HAIR

Round 1: Using **black**, 6 sc in a magic ring.

Round 2: 2 sc in each st. (12 sts)

Round 3: *1 sc, 2 sc in the next st; rep from * to end. (18 sts)

Round 4: *2 sc, 2 sc in the next st; rep from * to end. (24 sts)

Round 5: *3 sc, 2 sc in the next st; rep from * to end. (30 sts)

Round 6: *4 sc, 2 sc in the next st; rep from * to end. (36 sts)

Round 7: *5 sc, 2 sc in the next st; rep from * to end. (42 sts)

Round 8: *13 sc, 2 sc in the next st; rep from * to end. (45 sts)

Rounds 9 to 15: 1 sc in each st.

Round 16: 1 slst, 1 sc, 1 hdc, 10 dc, 1 hdc, 1 sc, 2 slst, *ch 11, 1 sc in second ch from hook, 1 sc in each st along ch (10 sts), 1 slst, rep from * to create 3 hair locks. Then 1 slst, 1 sc, 1 hdc, 10 dc, 1 hdc, 1 sc, 1 slst. Leave the rest of the stitches unworked.

Fasten off, leaving a long tail to sew to the head.

TIP

Sew the hair locks to Ella's hair and then curl them into place with your fingers.

EXTRA HAIR LOCKS (MAKE SIX)

Row 1: Using **black** and leaving a long initial tail, ch 16, 1 sc in the second ch from hook, 1 sc in each ch to end. (15 sts)

Fasten off, leaving a long tail to sew to the head.

FLOWER

For detailed photographs of how to work the flowers *see Techniques: Flowers*.

Round 1: Using **white**, 5 sc in a magic ring. (5 sts)

Round 2: *1 slst in the next st, ch 2 and yarn over, insert the hook into the same st, yarn over and pull yarn through the st. Yarn over, pull yarn through first 2 loops on your hook. Yarn over, insert hook into the same st, yarn over and pull yarn through the st. Yarn over, pull yarn through first 2 loops on your hook. Yarn over, pull yarn through the 3 remaining loops on hook, ch 2, 1 slst in same st to complete first petal. Repeat from * a further 4 times to make 5 petals; finish with 1 slst in the next st. (5 petals)

Fasten off, leaving a long tail to sew to the hair.

ASSEMBLY

Sew the hair onto the head (*see Techniques: Sewing the Hair*), with the three locks of hair over the forehead.

Sew the extra hair locks, two by two, in line with the three hair locks on the forehead and towards the back.

Sew the arms to the sides of the body (*see Techniques: Sewing the Arms*).

Sew the white flower to one of Ella's shoulders.

With the doll facing you and using **dark blue**, embroider one short straight line to mark the right edge of the skin colour triangle and one long line to mark the left edge all the way to the waist, as if it was a wrap dress.

Weave in all ends inside the doll.

"Where there is love and inspiration, I don't think you can go wrong."

2.5mm (C/2) crochet hook

100% 8-ply cotton; colours used: skin colour, white, light brown, dark old rose, dark grey, small amount of pink and of black

Yarn needle

Stitch marker

Fibrefill stuffing

FINISHED SIZE

19cm (7½in) tall

HELEN KELLER

Why Helen? Because she is a perfect example of resilience. In her early childhood she caught a strong fever that left her both blind and deaf. With the help of a one-of-a-kind teacher, and life-long friend, Anne Sullivan, she slowly learnt to speak and to read braille. She even studied several other languages, such as French, German, Latin and Greek, and was the first deaf-blind person to get a college degree – and she did so with high honours! Helen never gave up: she overcame every challenge, wrote books telling her story, and toured the world giving lectures and advocating for the rights of those with vision loss and other disabilities. She opened the eyes of the world to what people like her needed and made their voices heard.

LEG 1

Round 1: Using **skin** colour, 6 sc in a magic ring. (6 sts)

Round 2: 2 sc in each st. (12 sts)

Rounds 3 to 8: 1 sc in each st.

Round 9: Change to **white** for the underwear, 1 sc BLO in each st.

Fasten off invisibly (*see Techniques: Fasten Off Invisibly*) and weave in ends (*see Techniques: Weaving In Ends*). Set aside.

LEG 2

Work as for Leg 1, but do not fasten off yarn at the end. We will continue with the body.

BODY

Round 10: Still with leg 2 on your hook, ch 3 and join to leg 1 with a sc (*see Techniques: Joining Legs*), place a stitch marker here for new beg of round, work 11 sc all along leg 1, 1 sc into each ch of 3-ch-loop, 12 sc all along leg 2 and 1 sc into other side of each ch of 3-ch-loop. (30 sts)

Round 11: *4 sc, 2 sc in the next st, rep from * to end. (36 sts)

Rounds 12 to 16: 1 sc in each st.

Stuff the legs firmly at this point.

Round 17: *4 sc, sc2tog, rep from * to end. (30 sts)

Round 18: Change to **dark old rose** for the skirt, 1 sc in each st.

Round 19: Change to **dark grey** for the belt, 1 sc BLO in each st.

Round 20: *3 sc, sc2tog, rep from * to end. (24 sts)

Round 21: Change to **white** for the shirt, 1 sc BLO in each st.

Rounds 22 and 23: 1 sc in each st.

Start to stuff the body firmly at this point and continue to stuff as you work.

Round 24: *2 sc, sc2tog, rep from * to end. (18 sts)

Rounds 25 and 26: 1 sc in each st.

Round 27: *1 sc, sc2tog, rep from * to end. (12 sts)

Rounds 28 to 30: 1 sc in each st.

Round 31: Change to **skin** colour, 1 sc BLO in each st.

Do not fasten off yarn. We will continue with the head.

"Although the world is full of suffering, it is full also of the overcoming of it."

HEAD

Round 32: 2 sc in each st. (24 sts)

Round 33: *3 sc, 2 sc in the next st, rep from * to end. (30 sts)

Stuff the neck area firmly at this point.

Round 34: *4 sc, 2 sc in the next st, rep from * to end. (36 sts)

Round 35: *5 sc, 2 sc in the next st, rep from * to end. (42 sts)

Round 36: 1 sc in each st.

Round 37: 26 sc, 1 bobble st for the nose (*see Stitches: Bobble Stitch*), 1 sc in each st to end.

Be sure to align the nose with the middle of the legs and adjust the positioning if necessary.

We will take a break here from the head to work the collar of Helen's shirt. Place a stitch marker in the loop on your hook to secure it and cut the yarn.

COLLAR

Keep Helen's body head up and join **white** in one of the front loops of round 31, at the back of the neck.

Round 1: *1 sc FLO, 2 sc FLO in the next st; rep from * to end. (18 sts)

Round 2: *2 sc, 1 picot st (*see Stitches: Picot Stitch*) on top of the previous st, rep from * 8 more times, 1 slst in the first sc of the round to finish.

Fasten off invisibly and weave in ends.

We will now continue with the head. Rejoin the **skin** colour to where you stopped working the head.

Rounds 38 to 46: 1 sc in each st.

Round 47: *5 sc, sc2tog, rep from * to end. (36 sts)

Embroider closed eyes with **black**, with 8 sts between them, and embroider cheeks with **pink**.

Round 48: *4 sc, sc2tog, rep from * to end. (30 sts)

Start stuffing the head at this point.

Round 49: *3 sc, sc2tog, rep from * to end. (24 sts)

Round 50: *2 sc, sc2tog, rep from * to end. (18 sts)

Stuff firmly.

Round 51: *1 sc, sc2tog, rep from * to end. (12 sts)

Round 52: (Sc2tog) 6 times. (6 sts)

Fasten off and close the remaining stitches through the front loops (*see Techniques: Closing Remaining Stitches Through the Front Loops*). Weave in ends (*see Techniques: Hiding Ends Inside the Doll*).

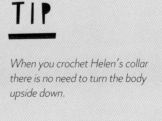

TIP

When you crochet Helen's collar there is no need to turn the body upside down.

TIP

Helen's skirt should touch the floor and cover her feet. To achieve this, feel free to add an extra straight round to the skirt.

SKIRT

Turn the body upside down and join **dark old rose** in one of the front loops of round 19, at the back of the body.

Round 1: 1 sc FLO in each st of round 19. (30 sts)

Round 2: *4 sc, 2 sc in the next st, rep from * to end. (36 sts)

Round 3: 1 sc in each st.

Round 4: *5 sc, 2 sc in the next st, rep from * to end. (42 sts)

Rounds 5 to 7: 1 sc in each st.

Round 8: *6 sc, 2 sc in the next st, rep from * to end. (48 sts)

Rounds 9 to 11: 1 sc in each st.

Round 12: Change to **dark grey**, 1 sc in each st.

Round 13: Change to **dark old rose**, 1 sc in each st.

Round 14: Change to **dark grey**, 1 sc in each st.

Round 15: *7 sc, 2 sc in the next st, rep from * to end. (54 sts)

Round 16: Change to **dark old rose**, 1 sc in each st.

Round 17: Change to **dark grey**, 1 sc in each st.

Rounds 18 and 19: 1 sc in each st.

Fasten off invisibly and weave in ends.

ARMS (MAKE TWO)

Round 1: Using **skin** colour, ch 2, 4 sc in the second ch from hook. (4 sts)

Round 2: 2 sc in each st. (8 sts)

Rounds 3 to 6: 1 sc in each st.

Round 7: Change to **white** for the shirt, 1 sc in each st.

Round 8: 1 sc BLO in each st.

Rounds 9 to 17: 1 sc in each st.

There is no need to stuff the arms.

Round 18: Press the opening with your fingers, aligning 4 sts side by side and sc both sides together by working 1 sc into each pair of sts (*see Techniques: Closing the Arms*).

Fasten off, leaving a long tail to sew to the body.

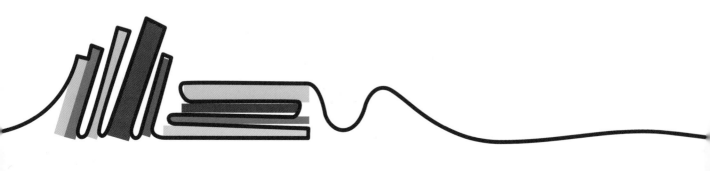

RUFFLES OF THE SLEEVES

Take one of the arms with the hand facing out and join **white** in one of the front loops of round 8.

Round 1: 2 sc FLO in each st of round 8. (16 sts)

Round 2: *2 sc, 1 picot st (*see Stitches: Picot Stitch*) on top of the previous st, rep from * 7 more times, 1 slst in the first sc of the round to finish.

Fasten off invisibly and weave in ends.

HAIR

Round 1: Using **light brown**, 6 sc in a magic ring.

Round 2: 2 sc in each st. (12 sts)

Round 3: *1 sc, 2 sc in the next st; rep from * to end. (18 sts)

Round 4: *2 sc, 2 sc in the next st; rep from * to end. (24 sts)

Round 5: *3 sc, 2 sc in the next st; rep from * to end. (30 sts)

Round 6: *4 sc, 2 sc in the next st; rep from * to end. (36 sts)

Round 7: *5 sc, 2 sc in the next st; rep from * to end. (42 sts)

Round 8: *13 sc, 2 sc in the next st; rep from * to end. (45 sts)

Rounds 9 to 15: 1 sc in each st.

Round 16: *Ch 13, 1 sc in second ch from hook, 1 sc in each st along ch (12 sts), 1 slst, rep from * to create 4 hair locks. Then 20 sc, ch 41, 1 sc in second ch from hook, 1 sc in each st along ch (40 sts), 1 slst.

Fasten off, leaving a long tail to sew to the head.

ASSEMBLY

Sew the hair onto the head (*see Techniques: Sewing the Hair*), with the four locks of hair on the forehead and the single long hair lock on the back. Part two short locks to each side of the forehead and secure them in place with a few stitches. Twist the long lock to create a low bun and secure the shape with a few stitches.

Sew the arms to the sides of the body (*see Techniques: Sewing the Arms*).

Weave in all ends inside the doll.

"The best and most beautiful things in the world cannot be seen or even touched. They must be felt with the heart."

MATERIALS

2.5mm (C/2) crochet hook

100% 8-ply cotton; colours used: skin colour, white, black, dark blue, yellow, light grey, small amount of pink

Yarn needle

8mm (⅓in) safety eyes

Stitch marker

Fibrefill stuffing

20cm (7¾in) of black coated wire

Round nose pliers

Plastic tube, approximately 1cm (⅜in) in diameter

Craft glue or black sewing thread

FINISHED SIZE

21cm (8¼in) tall

GRACE HOPPER

Why Grace? Because during World War II, she joined the American Navy and, thanks to her impressive brain, was able to understand the inner workings of the Harvard Mark 1, one of the earliest computers, which occupied an entire room, and explain it to others in an understandable language. Her skills at computer programming meant the Navy was able to solve important problems for the war effort. Due to her decades of work (she retired at age 79) and generous leadership, computing and coding became more accessible. It was her idea that computers should understand instructions written in English rather than complicated symbols so that anyone could learn to code. She is widely known as the Mother of Computing.

LEG 1

Round 1: Using **black** for the shoes, 6 sc in a magic ring. (6 sts)

Round 2: 2 sc in each st. (12 sts)

Round 3: 1 sc in each st.

Round 4: Change to **skin** colour, 1 sc BLO in each st.

Rounds 5 to 8: 1 sc in each st.

Round 9: Change to **white** for the underwear, 1 sc BLO in each st.

Fasten off invisibly (*see Techniques: Fasten Off Invisibly*) and weave in ends (*see Techniques: Weaving In Ends*). Set aside.

LEG 2

Work as for Leg 1, but do not fasten off yarn at the end. We will continue with the body.

BODY

Round 10: Still with leg 2 on your hook, 2 sc, ch 3 and join to leg 1 with a sc (*see Techniques: Joining Legs*), place a stitch marker here for new beg of round, work 11 sc all along leg 1, 1 sc into each ch of 3-ch-loop, 12 sc all along leg 2 and 1 sc into other side of each ch of 3-ch-loop. (30 sts)

Round 11: *4 sc, 2 sc in the next st, rep from * to end. (36 sts)

Rounds 12 to 15: 1 sc in each st.

Stuff the legs firmly at this point.

Round 16: Change to **dark blue** for the skirt, 1 sc in each st.

Round 17: 1 sc BLO in each st.

Round 18: *4 sc, sc2tog, rep from * to end. (30 sts)

Round 19: Change to **white** for the shirt, 1 sc BLO in each st.

Round 20: 1 sc in each st.

Round 21: *3 sc, sc2tog, rep from * to end. (24 sts)

Rounds 22 and 23: 1 sc in each st.

Start to stuff the body firmly at this point and continue to stuff as you work.

Round 24: *2 sc, sc2tog, rep from * to end. (18 sts)

Rounds 25 and 26: 1 sc in each st.

Round 27: *1 sc, sc2tog, rep from * to end. (12 sts)

Rounds 28 to 30: 1 sc in each st.

Round 31: Change to **skin** colour, 1 sc BLO in each st.

Round 32: 1 sc in each st.

Do not fasten off yarn. We will continue with the head.

HEAD

Round 33: 2 sc in each st. (24 sts)

Round 34: *3 sc, 2 sc in the next st, rep from * to end. (30 sts)

Stuff the neck area firmly at this point.

Round 35: *4 sc, 2 sc in the next st, rep from * to end. (36 sts)

Round 36: *5 sc, 2 sc in the next st, rep from * to end. (42 sts)

Round 37: 1 sc in each st.

Round 38: 26 sc, 1 bobble st for the nose (*see Stitches: Bobble Stitch*), 1 sc in each st to end.

Be sure to align the nose with the middle of the legs and adjust the positioning if necessary.

We will take a break here from the head to work the collar of Grace's shirt. Place a stitch marker in the loop on your hook to secure it and cut the yarn.

"If it's a good idea, go ahead and do it. It is much easier to apologize than it is to get permission."

COLLAR

For detailed photographs of how to work this collar *see Techniques: Making the Collars.*

Turn the body upside down and join **white** in one of the front loops of round 31, at the back of the neck.

Round 1: 1 sc FLO in each st of round 31. (12 sts)

Round 2: 4 sc, (1 hdc, 1 dc) in the next st, (3 dc) in the next st, 1 slst, (1 slst, ch 2, 2 dc) in the next st, (1 dc, 1 hdc) in the next st, 3 sc. (16 sts excluding slst and ch)

Fasten off invisibly and weave in ends.

We will now continue with the head. Rejoin the **skin** colour to where you stopped working the head.

Rounds 39 to 47: 1 sc in each st.

Round 48: *5 sc, sc2tog, rep from * to end. (36 sts)

Place safety eyes one round above the nose, with 8 sts between them (*see Techniques: Attaching Eyes*), embroider cheeks with **pink**.

Round 49: *4 sc, sc2tog, rep from * to end. (30 sts)

Start stuffing the head at this point.

Round 50: *3 sc, sc2tog, rep from * to end. (24 sts)

Round 51: *2 sc, sc2tog, rep from * to end. (18 sts)

Stuff firmly.

Round 52: *1 sc, sc2tog, rep from * to end. (12 sts)

Round 53: (Sc2tog) 6 times. (6 sts)

Fasten off and close the remaining stitches through the front loops (*see Techniques: Closing Remaining Stitches Through the Front Loops*). Weave in ends (*see Techniques: Hiding Ends Inside the Doll*).

SKIRT

Turn the body upside down and join **dark blue** in one of the front loops of round 17, at the back of the body.

Round 1: 1 sc FLO in each st of round 17. (36 sts)

Round 2: *5 sc, 2 sc in the next st, rep from * to end. (42 sts)

Rounds 3 and 4: 1 sc in each st.

Round 5: *6 sc, 2 sc in the next st, rep from * to end. (48 sts)

Rounds 6 to 9: 1 sc in each st.

Fasten off invisibly and weave in ends.

ARMS (MAKE TWO)

Round 1: Using **skin** colour, ch 2, 4 sc in the second ch from hook. (4 sts)

Round 2: 2 sc in each st. (8 sts)

Rounds 3 to 5: 1 sc in each st.

Round 6: Change to **dark blue** for the jacket, 1 sc BLO in each st.

Round 7: 1 sc in each st.

Round 8: Change to **yellow**, 1 sc in each st.

Round 9: 1 sc in each st.

Round 10: Change to **dark blue**, 1 sc in each st.

Rounds 11 to 17: 1 sc in each st.

There is no need to stuff the arms.

Round 18: Press the opening with your fingers, aligning 4 sts side by side and sc both sides together by working 1 sc into each pair of sts (*see Techniques: Closing the Arms*).

Fasten off, leaving a long tail to sew to the body.

TIP

The collar should be in line with the nose, so the slst on round 2 should sit right under it. If it isn't, unravel the round and add one or two sc when you begin!

JACKET

The jacket is actually a vest, but when you put it on your Grace, together with the arms, it will look like a jacket. The vest is worked in rows from the top down, using **dark blue**.

Row 1: Ch 21, 1 sc in the second ch from hook, 1 sc in each ch to end, ch 1, turn. (20 sts)

Row 2: 4 sc, *ch 6, skip the following 4 sts (to create armhole), 4 sc, rep from * once more, ch 1, turn.

Row 3: 4 sc, *6 sc in the 6-ch-loop, 4 sc, rep from * once more, ch 1, turn. (24 sts)

Rows 4 and 5: 1 sc in each st, ch 1, turn.

Row 6: 2 sc in the next st, 4 sc, 2 sc in the next st, 3 sc, 2 sc in the next st, 5 sc, 2 sc in the next st, 3 sc, 2 sc in the next st, 3 sc, 2 sc in the next st, ch 1, turn. (30 sts)

Row 7: 1 sc in each st, ch 1, turn.

Row 8: 2 sc in the next st, 5 sc, 2 sc in the next st, 6 sc, 2 sc in the next st, 3 sc, 2 sc in the next st, 6 sc, 2 sc in the next st, 4 sc, 2 sc in the next st, ch 1, turn. (36 sts)

Rows 9 to 12: 1 sc in each st, ch 1, turn.

Row 13: 1 sc in each st, ch 1, rotate the work 90 degrees clockwise and work 13 sc along the side of the vest, working in the spaces between rows. When you reach the top edge, crochet 20 sc in the remaining loops of the foundation chain. Then ch 1, rotate the piece 90 degrees clockwise again and work 13 sc along the other side of the vest, working in the spaces between rows (*see Techniques: Edging of Flat Pieces*).

Fasten off, leaving a long tail to sew and close the jacket.

HAIR

Round 1: Using **light grey**, 6 sc in a magic ring.

Round 2: 2 sc in each st. (12 sts)

Round 3: *1 sc, 2 sc in the next st; rep from * to end. (18 sts)

Round 4: *2 sc, 2 sc in the next st; rep from * to end. (24 sts)

Round 5: *3 sc, 2 sc in the next st; rep from * to end. (30 sts)

Round 6: *4 sc, 2 sc in the next st; rep from * to end. (36 sts)

Round 7: *5 sc, 2 sc in the next st; rep from * to end. (42 sts)

Round 8: *13 sc, 2 sc in the next st; rep from * to end. (45 sts)

Rounds 9 to 15: 1 sc in each st.

Round 16: 1 sc, 1 hdc, 10 dc, 1 hdc, 1 sc, 1 slst, 1 sc, 1 hdc, 10 dc, 1 hdc, 2 sc, *ch 6, 1 sc in second ch from hook, 1 sc in each st along ch (5 sts), 2 sc, rep from * to create 7 short hair locks. 1 slst in the last stitch of the round to finish.

Fasten off, leaving a long tail to sew to the head.

HAT

Round 1: Using **white** for the hat, 6 sc in a magic ring. (6 sts)

Round 2: 2 sc in each st. (12 sts)

Round 3: 2 sc in each st. (24 sts)

Round 4: *3 sc, 2 sc in the next st, rep from * to end. (30 sts)

Round 5: *4 sc, 2 sc in the next st, rep from * to end. (36 sts)

Round 6: *5 sc, 2 sc in the next st, rep from * to end. (42 sts)

Round 7: *6 sc, 2 sc in the next st, rep from * to end. (48 sts)

Round 8: 1 sc BLO in each st.

Rounds 9 to 13: 1 sc in each st.

Round 14: 1 sc BLO in each st.

Round 15: Change to **black**, 1 sc in each st.

Round 16: 1 sc in each st.

Fasten off invisibly and weave in ends.

RIM OF HAT

Turn the hat with the opening towards you and join **black** in one of the front loops of round 14 of the hat.

Round 1: 1 sc FLO in each st. (48 sts)

Round 2: 5 sc, 1 hdc, 4 dc, 4 tr, 4 dc, 1 hdc, 10 sc, 1 hdc, 4 dc, 4 tr, 4 dc, 1 hdc, 5 sc.

Fasten off invisibly and weave in ends.

BADGE

The badge is worked in rows, using **black**.

Row 1: Ch 6, 1 sc in the second ch from hook, 1 sc in each ch to end, ch 1, turn. (5 sts)

Rows 2 and 3: 1 sc in each st, ch 1, turn.

Row 4: 1 sc in each st, ch 1, rotate the work 90 degrees clockwise and work 4 sc along the side of the piece, working in the spaces between rows. When you reach the top edge, crochet 5 sc in the remaining loops of the foundation chain. Then ch 1, rotate the piece 90 degrees clockwise again and work 4 sc along the other side, working in the spaces between rows (see Techniques: Edging of Flat Pieces).

Fasten off invisibly, leaving a long tail to sew to the hat.

ASSEMBLY

Sew the hair to the head (see Techniques: Sewing the Hair).

Sew the arms to the sides of the body (see Techniques: Sewing the Arms).

Slip the vest onto Grace's arms. It will look like a jacket. Close it with a few stitches using the remaining yarn tail.

Sew the badge inside the rim of the hat.

With **yellow**, embroider three lines to the badge and two straight lines to the jacket to simulate Grace's military decorations.

Make Grace's glasses (see Techniques: Making Glasses) and use craft glue to stick glasses over the nose. You can also sew them using a bit of **black** thread.

Weave in all ends inside the doll.

TIP

Check the Stitches section to remind yourself how the triple crochet stitch is done.

FOR MARY

2.5mm (C/2) crochet hook

100% 8-ply cotton; colours used: skin colour, white, dark grey, light brown, small amount of pink

Yarn needle

8mm (⅓in) safety eyes

Stitch marker

Fibrefill stuffing

FOR FRANKENSTEIN'S MONSTER

2mm (B/1) crochet hook

100% 4-ply cotton; colours used: dark brown, light purple, mustard yellow, black

6mm (¼in) safety eyes

FINISHED SIZE

MARY

22.5cm (8¾in) tall

FRANKENSTEIN'S MONSTER

10cm (4in) tall

MARY SHELLEY

Why Mary? Because she was a brave and unique woman, different to young ladies of her time – free spirited, creative, a passionate reader, and much influenced by her mother Mary Wollstonecraft's writings about women's rights. During a stormy weekend at Lord Byron's a writing contest was proposed, and she conceived a story about the misuse of science and the consequences of the lack of love and the acceptance of appearances. *Frankenstein* was unlike anything written before and is considered an early example of science fiction. It was published anonymously in London in 1818 and many assumed her husband Percy was the author. In 1821 it was published again in Paris, in Mary's name, granting her the recognition she deserved.

LEG 1

Round 1: Using **skin** colour, 6 sc in a magic ring. (6 sts)

Round 2: 2 sc in each st. (12 sts)

Rounds 3 to 8: 1 sc in each st.

Round 9: Change to **white** for the underwear, 1 sc BLO in each st.

Fasten off invisibly (*see Techniques: Fasten Off Invisibly*) and weave in ends (*see Techniques: Weaving In Ends*). Set aside.

LEG 2

Work as for Leg 1, but do not fasten off yarn at the end. We will continue with the body.

BODY

Round 10: Still with leg 2 on your hook, ch 3 and join to leg 1 with a sc (*see Techniques: Joining Legs*), place a stitch marker here for new beg of round, work 11 sc all along leg 1, 1 sc into each ch of 3-ch-loop, 12 sc all along leg 2 and 1 sc into other side of each ch of 3-ch-loop. (30 sts)

Round 11: *4 sc, 2 sc in the next st, rep from * to end. (36 sts)

Rounds 12 to 16: 1 sc in each st.

Stuff the legs firmly at this point.

Round 17: *4 sc, sc2tog, rep from * to end. (30 sts)

Round 18: Change to **dark grey** for the skirt, 1 sc in each st.

Round 19: Change to **white** for the belt, 1 sc BLO in each st.

Round 20: *3 sc, sc2tog, rep from * to end. (24 sts)

Round 21: Change to **dark grey**, 1 sc BLO in each st.

Rounds 22 and 23: 1 sc in each st.

Start to stuff the body firmly at this point and continue to stuff as you work.

Round 24: *2 sc, sc2tog, rep from * to end. (18 sts)

Rounds 25 and 26: 1 sc in each st.

Round 27: Change to **white**, 1 sc in each st.

Round 28: Change to **skin** colour, 1 sc BLO in each st.

Round 29: *1 sc, sc2tog, rep from * to end. (12 sts)

Rounds 30 to 32: 1 sc in each st.

Do not fasten off yarn. We will continue with the head.

HEAD

Round 33: 2 sc in each st. (24 sts)

Round 34: *3 sc, 2 sc in the next st, rep from * to end. (30 sts)

Stuff the neck area firmly at this point.

Round 35: *4 sc, 2 sc in the next st, rep from * to end. (36 sts)

Round 36: *5 sc, 2 sc in the next st, rep from * to end. (42 sts)

Round 37: 1 sc in each st.

Round 38: 26 sc, 1 bobble st for the nose (*see Stitches: Bobble Stitch*), 1 sc in each st to end.

Be sure to align the nose with the middle of the legs and adjust the positioning if necessary.

Rounds 39 to 47: 1 sc in each st.

Round 48: *5 sc, sc2tog, rep from * to end. (36 sts)

Place safety eyes one round above the nose, with 8 sts between them (*see Techniques: Attaching Eyes*), embroider cheeks with **pink**.

Round 49: *4 sc, sc2tog, rep from * to end. (30 sts)

Start stuffing the head at this point.

Round 50: *3 sc, sc2tog, rep from * to end. (24 sts)

Round 51: *2 sc, sc2tog, rep from * to end. (18 sts)

Stuff firmly.

"Nothing contributes so much to tranquilize the mind as a steady purpose."

Round 52: *1 sc, sc2tog, rep from * to end. (12 sts)

Round 53: (Sc2tog) 6 times. (6 sts)

Fasten off and close the remaining stitches through the front loops (*see Techniques: Closing Remaining Stitches Through the Front Loops*). Weave in ends (*see Techniques: Hiding Ends Inside the Doll*).

COLLAR

Turn the body upside down and join **white** in one of the front loops of round 28, at the back of the body.

Round 1: 1 sc FLO in each st of round 28. (18 sts)

Round 2: *2 sc, 2 sc in the next st, rep from * to end. (24 sts)

Round 3: *2 sc, 1 picot st (*see Stitches: Picot Stitch*) on top of the previous st, rep from * to end, 1 slst in the first sc of the round to finish.

Fasten off invisibly and weave in ends.

SKIRT

Turn the body upside down and join **dark grey** in one of the front loops of round 19, at the back of the body.

Round 1: 1 sc FLO in each st of round 19. (30 sts)

Round 2: *4 sc, 2 sc in the next st, rep from * to end. (36 sts)

Round 3: 1 sc in each st.

Round 4: *5 sc, 2 sc in the next st, rep from * to end. (42 sts)

Rounds 5 to 7: 1 sc in each st.

Round 8: *6 sc, 2 sc in the next st, rep from * to end. (48 sts)

Rounds 9 to 11: 1 sc in each st.

Round 12: *7 sc, 2 sc in the next st, rep from * to end. (54 sts)

Rounds 13 to 16: 1 sc in each st.

Round 17: *8 sc, 2 sc in the next st, rep from * to end. (60 sts)

Rounds 18 and 19: 1 sc in each st.

Fasten off invisibly and weave in ends.

ARMS (MAKE TWO)

Round 1: Using **skin** colour, ch 2, 4 sc in the second ch from hook. (4 sts)

Round 2: 2 sc in each st. (8 sts)

Rounds 3 to 5: 1 sc in each st.

Round 6: Change to **dark grey** for the dress, 1 sc BLO in each st.

Rounds 7 to 16: 1 sc in each st.

There is no need to stuff the arms.

Round 17: Press the opening with your fingers, aligning 4 sts side by side and sc both sides together by working 1 sc into each pair of sts (*see Techniques: Closing the Arms*).

Fasten off, leaving a long tail to sew to the body.

HAIR

Round 1: Using **light brown**, 6 sc in a magic ring.

Round 2: 2 sc in each st. (12 sts)

Round 3: *1 sc, 2 sc in the next st; rep from * to end. (18 sts)

Round 4: *2 sc, 2 sc in the next st; rep from * to end. (24 sts)

Round 5: *3 sc, 2 sc in the next st; rep from * to end. (30 sts)

Round 6: *4 sc, 2 sc in the next st; rep from * to end. (36 sts)

Round 7: *5 sc, 2 sc in the next st; rep from * to end. (42 sts)

Round 8: *13 sc, 2 sc in the next st; rep from * to end. (45 sts)

Rounds 9 to 15: 1 sc in each st.

Round 16: *Ch 21, 2 sc in second ch from hook, 2 sc in each st along ch (40 sts), 2 slst, rep from * once more, 1 sc, 1 hdc, 8 dc, 1 hdc, 1 sc, 1 slst, 1 sc, 1 hdc, 8 dc, 1 hdc, 1 sc, 2 slst, **ch 21, 2 sc in second ch from hook, 2 sc in each st along ch (40 sts), 2 slst, rep from ** once more. Leave the rest of the stitches unworked.

Fasten off, leaving a long tail to sew to the head.

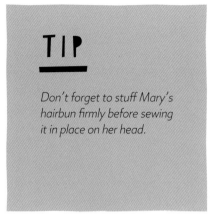

TIP

Don't forget to stuff Mary's hairbun firmly before sewing it in place on her head.

HAIRBUN

Round 1: Using **light brown**, 6 sc in a magic ring. (6 sts)

Round 2: 2 sc in each st. (12 sts)

Round 3: *1 sc, 2 sc in the next st, rep from * to end. (18 sts)

Rounds 4 to 7: 1 sc in each st.

Round 8: *1 sc, sc2tog, rep from * to end. (12 sts)

Fasten off, leaving a long tail to sew to the head.

ASSEMBLY

Sew the hair onto the head (*see Techniques: Sewing the Hair*), with the curls to the sides.

Stuff the hairbun and sew it to the head.

Lift the white collar and sew the arms to the sides of the body, right below the collar (*see Techniques: Sewing the Arms*).

Weave in all ends inside the doll.

FRANKENSTEIN'S MONSTER

IMPORTANT! The monster is crocheted using the smaller hook size of 2mm (US B/1) and the 4-ply yarn.

LEG 1

Round 1: Using **dark brown**, 5 sc in a magic ring. (5 sts)

Round 2: 2 sc in each st. (10 sts)

Round 3: 1 sc BLO in each st.

Rounds 4 and 5: 1 sc in each st.

Fasten off invisibly and weave in ends. Set aside.

LEG 2

Work as for Leg 1, but do not fasten off yarn at the end. We will continue with the body.

BODY

Round 6: Still with leg 2 on your hook, ch 2 and join to leg 1 with a sc (*see Techniques: Joining Legs*), place a stitch marker here for new beg of round, work 9 sc all along leg 1, 1 sc into each ch of 2-ch-loop, 10 sc all along leg 2 and 1 sc into other side of each ch of 2-ch-loop. (24 sts)

Rounds 7 to 11: 1 sc in each st.

Stuff the legs firmly at this point.

Round 12: Change to **light purple** for the shirt, 1 sc BLO in each st.

Round 13: *2 sc, sc2tog, rep from * to end. (18 sts)

Rounds 14 to 16: 1 sc in each st.

Stuff the body firmly at this point.

Round 17: *1 sc, sc2tog, rep from * to end. (12 sts)

Rounds 18 to 20: 1 sc in each st.

Round 21: Change to **mustard yellow** for the skin, 1 sc BLO in each st.

Do not fasten off yarn. We will continue with the head.

HEAD

Round 22: 2 sc in each st. (24 sts)

Round 23: *1 sc, 2 sc in the next st, rep from * to end. (36 sts)

Stuff the neck area firmly at this point.

Rounds 24 to 36: 1 sc in each st.

Place safety eyes between rounds 26 and 27, with 7 sts between them, embroider cheeks with **light purple**.

Fasten off invisibly and weave in ends.

EARS (MAKE TWO)

Round 1: Using **skin** colour, 6 sc in a magic ring. (6 sts)

Close the ring with a slst into the first sc and fasten off, leaving a long tail to sew to the head.

HAIR

Round 1: Using **black**, 6 sc in a magic ring. (6 sts)

Round 2: 2 sc in each st. (12 sts)

Round 3: 2 sc in each st. (24 sts)

Round 4: *3 sc, 2 sc in the next st, rep from * to end. (30 sts)

Round 5: *4 sc, 2 sc in the next st, rep from * to end. (36 sts)

Round 6: *8 sc, 2 sc in the next st, rep from * to end. (40 sts)

Round 7: 1 sc in each st.

Round 8: 1 sc BLO in each st.

Round 9: 1 sc in each st.

Round 10: *Ch 4, 1 sc in second ch from hook, 1 sc in each st along ch (3 sts), 5 sc, ch 3, 1 sc in second ch from hook, 1 sc in each st along ch (2 sts), 5 sc, rep from * 3 more times.

Fasten off, leaving a long tail to sew to the head.

ARMS (MAKE TWO)

Round 1: Using **mustard yellow**, ch 2, 4 sc in the second ch from hook. (4 sts)

Round 2: 2 sc in each st. (8 sts)

Rounds 3 to 9: 1 sc in each st.

Round 10: Change to **light purple** for the shirt, 1 sc BLO in each st.

Rounds 11 and 12: 1 sc in each st.

There is no need to stuff the arms.

Round 13: Press the opening with your fingers, aligning 4 sts side by side and sc both sides together by working 1 sc into each pair of sts (*see Techniques: Closing the Arms*).

Fasten off, leaving a long tail to sew to the body.

ASSEMBLY

Stuff the head firmly and sew the hair as a flat top (*see Techniques: Sewing the Hair*), securing the locks to the forehead with a few stitches.

Sew the ears to the sides of the head.

Sew the arms to the sides of the body (*see Techniques: Sewing the Arms*).

Using **light purple**, embroider a tiny scar to his forehead, slightly off centre.

Weave in all ends inside the doll.

MATERIALS

2.5mm (C/2) crochet hook

100% 8-ply cotton; colours used: skin colour, white, black, small amount of pink

Yarn needle

8mm (⅓in) safety eyes

Stitch marker

Fibrefill stuffing

White tulle

FINISHED SIZE

22cm (8½in) tall

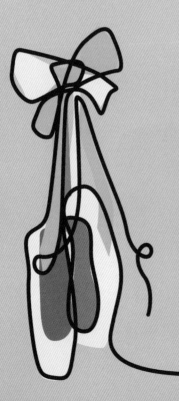

MISTY COPELAND

Why Misty? Because she was the first African-American to be made principal dancer at the American Ballet Theatre in New York City, one of the greatest companies in the world. Despite her humble beginnings and having started ballet training at a late age, it was easy to see Misty had potential and she was able to thrive and bloom in such a competitive world. She has become an icon, proving that ballerinas can have different yet positive body shapes and encouraging other dancers to embrace their uniqueness. Conscious of the difficulties fellow artists faced to reach their dreams, she uses her spotlight to mentor dancers like herself and to introduce ballet to wider audiences, becoming a symbol of diversity and change.

TIP

When joining the legs, make sure the colour changes in the first leg face you, so they will remain in the back of Misty's body.

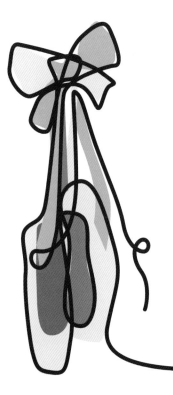

LEG 1

Round 1: Using **white** for the ballet shoes, 6 sc in a magic ring. (6 sts)

Round 2: 2 sc in each st. (12 sts)

Round 3: 1 sc in each st.

Round 4: Change to **skin** colour, 1 sc BLO in each st.

Rounds 5 to 8: 1 sc in each st.

Round 9: Change to **white** for the underwear, 1 sc BLO in each st.

Fasten off invisibly (*see Techniques: Fasten Off Invisibly*) and weave in ends (*see Techniques: Weaving In Ends*). Set aside.

LEG 2

Work as for Leg 1, but do not fasten off yarn at the end. We will continue with the body.

BODY

Round 10: Still with leg 2 on your hook, 2 sc, ch 3 and join to leg 1 with a sc (*see Techniques: Joining Legs*), place a stitch marker here for new beg of round, work 11 sc all along leg 1, 1 sc into each ch of 3-ch-loop, 12 sc all along leg 2 and 1 sc into other side of each ch of 3-ch-loop. (30 sts)

Round 11: *4 sc, 2 sc in the next st, rep from * to end. (36 sts)

Rounds 12 to 16: 1 sc in each st.

Stuff the legs firmly at this point.

Round 17: *4 sc, sc2tog, rep from * to end. (30 sts)

Round 18: 1 sc BLO in each st.

Round 19: 1 sc in each st.

Round 20: *3 sc, sc2tog, rep from * to end. (24 sts)

Rounds 21 to 23: 1 sc in each st.

Start to stuff the body firmly at this point and continue to stuff as you work.

Round 24: *2 sc, sc2tog, rep from * to end. (18 sts)

Round 25: Change to **skin** colour, 1 sc BLO in each st.

Round 26: 1 sc in each st.

Round 27: *1 sc, sc2tog, rep from * to end. (12 sts)

Rounds 28 to 31: 1 sc in each st.

Do not fasten off yarn. We will continue with the head.

HEAD

Round 32: 2 sc in each st. (24 sts)

Round 33: *3 sc, 2 sc in the next st, rep from * to end. (30 sts)

Stuff the neck area firmly at this point.

Round 34: *4 sc, 2 sc in the next st, rep from * to end. (36 sts)

Round 35: *5 sc, 2 sc in the next st, rep from * to end. (42 sts)

Round 36: 1 sc in each st.

Round 37: 26 sc, 1 bobble st for the nose (*see Stitches: Bobble Stitch*), 1 sc in each st to end.

Be sure to align the nose with the middle of the legs and adjust the positioning if necessary.

Rounds 38 to 46: 1 sc in each st.

Round 47: *5 sc, sc2tog, rep from * to end. (36 sts)

Place safety eyes one round above the nose, with 8 sts between them (*see Techniques: Attaching Eyes*), embroider cheeks with **pink**.

Round 48: *4 sc, sc2tog, rep from * to end. (30 sts)

Start stuffing the head at this point.

Round 49: *3 sc, sc2tog, rep from * to end. (24 sts)

Round 50: *2 sc, sc2tog, rep from * to end. (18 sts)

Stuff firmly.

Round 51: *1 sc, sc2tog, rep from * to end. (12 sts)

Round 52: (Sc2tog) 6 times. (6 sts)

Fasten off and close the remaining stitches through the front loops (*see Techniques: Closing Remaining Stitches Through the Front Loops*). Weave in ends (*see Techniques: Hiding Ends Inside the Doll*).

ARMS (MAKE TWO)

Round 1: Using **skin** colour, ch 2, 4 sc in the second ch from hook. (4 sts)

Round 2: 2 sc in each st. (8 sts)

Rounds 3 to 17: 1 sc in each st.

There is no need to stuff the arms.

Round 18: Press the opening with your fingers, aligning 4 sts side by side and sc both sides together by working 1 sc into each pair of sts (*see Techniques: Closing the Arms*).

Fasten off, leaving a long tail to sew to the body.

"Promote yourself. If you don't think you're worthy, you're never going to make it."

STRAP FOR THE BALLET DRESS

Row 1: Using **white** and leaving a long initial tail, ch 20.

Fasten off, leaving a long tail to sew around the neck.

HAIR

Round 1: Using **black**, 6 sc in a magic ring.

Round 2: 2 sc in each st. (12 sts)

Round 3: *1 sc, 2 sc in the next st; rep from * to end. (18 sts)

Round 4: *2 sc, 2 sc in the next st; rep from * to end. (24 sts)

Round 5: *3 sc, 2 sc in the next st; rep from * to end. (30 sts)

Round 6: *4 sc, 2 sc in the next st; rep from * to end. (36 sts)

Round 7: *5 sc, 2 sc in the next st; rep from * to end. (42 sts)

Round 8: *13 sc, 2 sc in the next st; rep from * to end. (45 sts)

Rounds 9 to 15: 1 sc in each st.

Round 16: 1 slst, 1 sc, 1 hdc, 10 dc, 1 hdc, 1 sc, 1 slst, 1 sc, 1 hdc, 10 dc, 1 hdc, 1 sc, 1 slst. Leave the rest of the stitches unworked.

Fasten off, leaving a long tail to sew to the head.

HAIRBUN

Round 1: Using **black**, 5 sc in a magic ring. (5 sts)

Round 2: 2 sc in each st. (10 sts)

Round 3: *1 sc, 2 sc in the next st, rep from * to end. (15 sts)

Round 4: *2 sc, 2 sc in the next st, rep from * to end. (20 sts)

Rounds 5 to 7: 1 sc in each st.

Round 8: *2 sc, sc2tog, rep from * to end. (15 sts)

Round 9: Change to **white**, 1 sc in each st.

Fasten off, leaving a long tail to sew to the head.

FLOWERS (MAKE TWO)

For detailed photographs of how to work the flowers *see Techniques: Flowers*.

Round 1: Using **white**, 5 sc in a magic ring. (5 sts)

Round 2: *1 slst in the next st, ch 2 and yarn over, insert the hook into the same st, yarn over and pull yarn through the st. Yarn over, pull yarn through first 2 loops on your hook. Yarn over, insert hook into the same st, yarn over and pull yarn through the st. Yarn over, pull yarn through first 2 loops on your hook. Yarn over, pull yarn through the 3 remaining loops on hook, ch 2, 1 slst in same st to complete first petal. Repeat from * a further 4 times to make 5 petals; finish with 1 slst in the next st. (5 petals)

Fasten off, leaving a long tail to sew to the hair.

TULLE SKIRT

Cut 60 pieces of tulle of approximately 15cm (6in) long and 1.5cm (½in) wide. Grab 2 pieces of tulle at their middle and pull a loop halfway through one of the white remaining front loops on round 18 of Misty's body. Then insert the ends of the tulle pieces into the loop to secure the knot. Repeat this with all the front loops of the round, to complete the tulle skirt. Finally trim all the ends to the desired length.

ASSEMBLY

Sew the hair onto the head (*see Techniques: Sewing the Hair*).

Stuff the hairbun and sew it to the head.

Sew the flowers to one side of the hairbun.

Sew the arms to the sides of the body (*see Techniques: Sewing the Arms*).

Sew the strap of the ballet dress in the middle of the front of the chest, around the neck and back into the middle of the chest.

Using **white**, make laces to the ballet shoes.

Weave in all ends inside the doll.

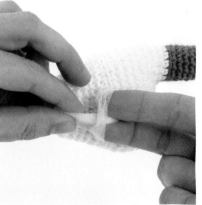

"Be strong, be fearless, be beautiful. And believe that anything is possible when you have the right people there to support you."

TIP

If your tulle is too thin, you can use three or four pieces to pull through each front loop to make the tutu thicker.

MATERIALS

2.5mm (C/2) crochet hook

100% 8-ply cotton; colours used: skin colour, white, dark brown, sunny yellow, small amount of pink

Yarn needle

8mm (⅓in) safety eyes

Stitch marker

Fibrefill stuffing

FINISHED SIZE

19cm (7½in) tall

HYPATIA
OF ALEXANDRIA

Why Hypatia? Because she is known as the first female mathematician in recorded history; she was also an astronomer, a philosopher, an educator and one of the last great thinkers of Alexandria, in Egypt. She wrote important works on geometry and numbers and also held public classes, even teaching students how to design tools to study the stars! She also gave lectures about the work of philosophers like Plato and Aristotle and people came from afar just to listen to her. But some of her teaching was considered 'pagan' at the time, and she was killed by an angry mob who burnt her body. Her violent death, an example of religious extremism, turned Hypatia into a symbol of tolerance and respect for others.

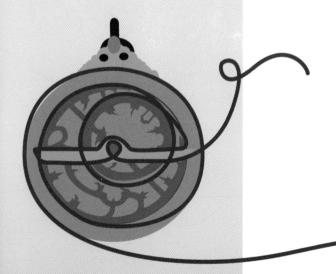

LEG 1

Round 1: Using **skin** colour, 6 sc in a magic ring. (6 sts)

Round 2: 2 sc in each st. (12 sts)

Rounds 3 to 8: 1 sc in each st.

Round 9: Change to **white** for the underwear, 1 sc BLO in each st.

Fasten off invisibly (*see Techniques: Fasten Off Invisibly*) and weave in ends (*see Techniques: Weaving In Ends*). Set aside.

LEG 2

Work as for Leg 1, but do not fasten off yarn at the end. We will continue with the body.

BODY

Round 10: Still with leg 2 on your hook, ch 3 and join to leg 1 with a sc (*see Techniques: Joining Legs*), place a stitch marker here for new beg of round, work 11 sc all along leg 1, 1 sc into each ch of 3-ch-loop, 12 sc all along leg 2 and 1 sc into other side of each ch of 3-ch-loop. (30 sts)

Round 11: *4 sc, 2 sc in the next st, rep from * to end. (36 sts)

Rounds 12 to 16: 1 sc in each st.

Stuff the legs firmly at this point.

Round 17: *4 sc, sc2tog, rep from * to end. (30 sts)

Round 18: 1 sc in each st.

Round 19: Change to **sunny yellow** for the belt, 1 sc BLO in each st.

Round 20: *3 sc, sc2tog, rep from * to end. (24 sts)

Round 21: Change back to **white**, 1 sc BLO in each st.

Rounds 22 and 23: 1 sc in each st.

Start to stuff the body firmly at this point and continue to stuff as you work.

Round 24: *2 sc, sc2tog, rep from * to end. (18 sts)

Rounds 25 and 26: 1 sc in each st.

Round 27: *1 sc, sc2tog, rep from * to end. (12 sts)

Round 28: 1 sc in each st.

Round 29: Change to **skin** colour, 1 sc BLO in each st.

Rounds 30 and 31: 1 sc in each st.

Do not fasten off yarn. We will continue with the head.

HEAD

Round 32: 2 sc in each st. (24 sts)

Round 33: *3 sc, 2 sc in the next st, rep from * to end. (30 sts)

Stuff the neck area firmly at this point.

Round 34: *4 sc, 2 sc in the next st, rep from * to end. (36 sts)

Round 35: *5 sc, 2 sc in the next st, rep from * to end. (42 sts)

Round 36: 1 sc in each st.

Round 37: 26 sc, 1 bobble st for the nose (*see Stitches: Bobble Stitch*), 1 sc in each st to end.

Be sure to align the nose with the middle of the legs and adjust the positioning if necessary.

Rounds 38 to 46: 1 sc in each st.

Round 47: *5 sc, sc2tog, rep from * to end. (36 sts)

Place safety eyes one round above the nose, with 8 sts between them, and embroider cheeks with **pink**.

Round 48: *4 sc, sc2tog, rep from * to end. (30 sts)

Start stuffing the head at this point.

Round 49: *3 sc, sc2tog, rep from * to end. (24 sts)

Round 50: *2 sc, sc2tog, rep from * to end. (18 sts)

Stuff firmly.

Round 51: *1 sc, sc2tog, rep from * to end. (12 sts)

Round 52: (Sc2tog) 6 times. (6 sts)

Fasten off and close the remaining stitches through the front loops (*see Techniques: Closing Remaining Stitches Through the Front Loops*). Weave in ends (*see Techniques: Hiding Ends Inside the Doll*).

PLEATED SKIRT

Turn the doll's body upside down and join **white** with a slip knot in one of the front loops of round 19 at the back of the body.

Ch 19, 1 sc in the second ch from hook, 1 sc in each ch to end (18 sc), *1 slst in next front loop of round 19, turn, 1 sc BLO in each st of skirt, ch 1, turn, 1 sc BLO in each st to end (18 sc); rep from * until each st from round 19 has been worked.

Fasten off, leaving a long tail to sew the seam.

Thread your yarn needle with the remaining yarn tail and sew both sides of the skirt together.

"Reserve your right to think, for even to think wrongly is better than not to think at all."

TIP

Secure the drape in place by only sewing the tip of the ends. There is no need to sew it from her shoulder.

ARMS (MAKE TWO)

Round 1: Using **skin** colour, ch 2, 4 sc in the second ch from hook. (4 sts)

Round 2: 2 sc in each st. (8 sts)

Rounds 3 to 17: 1 sc in each st.

There is no need to stuff the arms.

Round 18: Press the opening with your fingers, aligning 4 sts side by side and sc both sides together by working 1 sc into each pair of sts (*see Techniques: Closing the Arms*).

Fasten off, leaving a long tail to sew to the body.

TUNIC DRAPE

The drape is crocheted in rows.

Row 1: Using **white**, ch 51, 1 sc in the second ch from hook, 1 sc in each ch to end. (50 sts)

Rows 2 to 5: Ch 1, turn, 1 sc BLO in each st.

Fasten off and weave in ends.

"Life is an unfoldment, and the further we travel the more truth we can comprehend."

HAIR

Round 1: Using **dark brown**, 6 sc in a magic ring.

Round 2: 2 sc in each st. (12 sts)

Round 3: *1 sc, 2 sc in the next st; rep from * to end. (18 sts)

Round 4: *2 sc, 2 sc in the next st; rep from * to end. (24 sts)

Round 5: *3 sc, 2 sc in the next st; rep from * to end. (30 sts)

Round 6: *4 sc, 2 sc in the next st; rep from * to end. (36 sts)

Round 7: *5 sc, 2 sc in the next st; rep from * to end. (42 sts)

Round 8: *13 sc, 2 sc in the next st; rep from * to end. (45 sts)

Rounds 9 to 15: 1 sc in each st.

Round 16: 1 slst, *ch 36, 1 sc in second ch from hook, 1 sc in each st along ch (35 sts), 1 slst; rep from * once more, 13 sc, **2 sc, ch 21, 1 sc in second ch from hook, 1 sc in each st along ch (20 sts); rep from ** to create 8 hair locks. 1 slst to finish. Leave the rest of the stitches of the round unworked.

Fasten off, leaving a long tail to sew to the head.

HAIRBUN

Round 1: Using **dark brown**, 6 sc in a magic ring.

Round 2: 2 sc in each st. (12 sts)

Round 3: *1 sc, 2 sc in the next st; rep from * to end. (18 sts)

Rounds 4 to 7: 1 sc in each st.

Fasten off, leaving a long tail to sew to the head.

HEADBAND (MAKE TWO)

Row 1: Using **sunny yellow** and leaving a long initial tail, ch 36.

Fasten off, leaving a long tail to sew to the head.

ASSEMBLY

Sew the hair onto the head (*see Techniques: Sewing the Hair*), with the two long locks of hair on the forehead. Do not sew these locks yet. First sew the two headbands to the head using the yarn tails. Now part the two long hair locks one to each side and sew them right over where the headbands meet.

Stuff the hairbun and sew it to the head. Wrap it witth a length of **sunny yellow**.

Sew the arms to the sides of the body (*see Techniques: Sewing the Arms*).

Cover one shoulder with the drape and sew one of the corners together.

Weave in all ends inside the doll.

2.5mm (C/2) crochet hook

100% 8-ply cotton; colours used: skin colour, white, light blue, light yellow, light grey, small amount of pink

Yarn needle

8mm (⅓in) safety eyes

Stitch marker

Fibrefill stuffing

Silver embroidery thread (optional)

Plastic pearl beads

Transparent beading cord

FINISHED SIZE

20cm (7¾in) tall

DIANA, PRINCESS OF WALES

Why Diana? Because when she became a princess, she used her fame to help people and redirected her spotlight to many issues that truly mattered, like the treatment of patients with cancer and AIDS. She redefined the role of a working royal and was affectionate, honest and caring, always ready to give a hug, offer a listening ear or simply share a comforting smile. She was never reluctant to go near those needing her attention and even kneel to listen to them closely. No wonder she became known as the People's Princess. She had a huge impact on those she met personally and the many others who followed her on the news. Her legacy of compassion lives on in the way her sons have embraced the causes that were important to her.

LEG 1

Round 1: Using **skin** colour, 6 sc in a magic ring. (6 sts)

Round 2: 2 sc in each st. (12 sts)

Rounds 3 to 8: 1 sc in each st.

Round 9: Change to **white** for the underwear, 1 sc BLO in each st.

Fasten off invisibly (*see Techniques: Fasten Off Invisibly*) and weave in ends (*see Techniques: Weaving In Ends*). Set aside.

LEG 2

Work as for Leg 1, but do not fasten off yarn at the end. We will continue with the body.

BODY

Round 10: Still with leg 2 on your hook, ch 3 and join to leg 1 with a sc (*see Techniques: Joining Legs*), place a stitch marker here for new beg of round, work 11 sc all along leg 1, 1 sc into each ch of 3-ch-loop, 12 sc all along leg 2 and 1 sc into other side of each ch of 3-ch-loop. (30 sts)

Round 11: *4 sc, 2 sc in the next st, rep from * to end. (36 sts)

Rounds 12 to 16: 1 sc in each st.

Stuff the legs firmly at this point.

Round 17: *4 sc, sc2tog, rep from * to end. (30 sts)

Round 18: Change to **light blue**, 1 sc in each st.

Round 19: 1 sc BLO in each st.

Round 20: *3 sc, sc2tog, rep from * to end. (24 sts)

Rounds 21 to 23: 1 sc in each st.

Round 24: *2 sc, sc2tog, rep from * to end. (18 sts)

Stuff the body firmly at this point.

Rounds 25 and 26: 1 sc in each st.

Round 27: Change to **skin** colour, 1 sc BLO in each st.

Round 28: *1 sc, sc2tog, rep from * to end. (12 sts)

Rounds 29 to 32: 1 sc in each st.

Do not fasten off yarn. We will continue with the head.

"Everyone needs to be valued. Everyone has the potential to give something back."

HEAD

Round 33: 2 sc in each st. (24 sts)

Round 34: *3 sc, 2 sc in the next st, rep from * to end. (30 sts)

Stuff the neck area firmly at this point.

Round 35: *4 sc, 2 sc in the next st, rep from * to end. (36 sts)

Round 36: *5 sc, 2 sc in the next st, rep from * to end. (42 sts)

Round 37: 1 sc in each st.

Round 38: 26 sc, 1 bobble st for the nose (see Stitches: Bobble Stitch), 1 sc in each st to end.

Be sure to align the nose with the middle of the legs and adjust the positioning if necessary.

Rounds 39 to 47: 1 sc in each st.

Round 48: *5 sc, sc2tog, rep from * to end. (36 sts)

Place safety eyes one round above the nose, with 8 sts between them (see Techniques: Attaching Eyes), embroider cheeks with **pink**.

Round 49: *4 sc, sc2tog, rep from * to end. (30 sts)

Start stuffing the head at this point.

Round 50: *3 sc, sc2tog, rep from * to end. (24 sts)

Round 51: *2 sc, sc2tog, rep from * to end. (18 sts)

Stuff firmly.

Round 52: *1 sc, sc2tog, rep from * to end. (12 sts)

Round 53: (Sc2tog) 6 times. (6 sts)

Fasten off and close the remaining stitches through the front loops (see Techniques: Closing Remaining Stitches Through the Front Loops). Weave in ends (see Techniques: Hiding Ends Inside the Doll).

SKIRT OF DRESS

Turn the body upside down and join **light blue** in one of the front loops of round 19, at the back of the body.

Round 1: 1 sc FLO in each st of round 19. (30 sts)

Round 2: *4 sc, 2 sc in the next st, rep from * to end. (36 sts)

Round 3: 1 sc in each st.

Round 4: *5 sc, 2 sc in the next st, rep from * to end. (42 sts)

Rounds 5 to 7: 1 sc in each st.

Round 8: *6 sc, 2 sc in the next st, rep from * to end. (48 sts)

Rounds 9 to 14: 1 sc in each st.

Round 15: *7 sc, 2 sc in the next st, rep from * to end. (54 sts)

Rounds 16 to 20: 1 sc in each st.

Fasten off invisibly and weave in ends.

ARMS (MAKE TWO)

Round 1: Using **skin** colour, ch 2, 4 sc in the second ch from hook. (4 sts)

Round 2: 2 sc in each st. (8 sts)

Rounds 3 to 9: 1 sc in each st.

Round 10: Change to **light blue** for the jacket, 1 sc BLO in each st.

Rounds 11 to 17: 1 sc in each st.

There is no need to stuff the arms.

Round 18: Press the opening with your fingers, aligning 4 sts side by side and sc both sides together by working 1 sc into each pair of sts (see Techniques: Closing the Arms).

Fasten off, leaving a long tail to sew to the body.

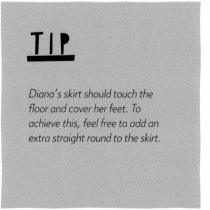

TIP

Diana's skirt should touch the floor and cover her feet. To achieve this, feel free to add an extra straight round to the skirt.

JACKET

The jacket is actually a vest, but when you put it on your doll, together with the arms, it will look like a jacket. The vest is worked in rows from the top down, using **light blue**.

Row 1: Ch 21, 1 sc in the second ch from hook, 1 sc in each ch to end, ch 1, turn. (20 sts)

Rows 2 to 4: 1 sc in each st, ch 1, turn.

Row 5: 4 sc, *ch 6, skip the following 4 sts (to create armhole), 4 sc, rep from * once more, ch 1, turn.

Row 6: 4 sc, *6 sc in the 6-ch-loop, 4 sc, rep from * once more, ch 1, turn. (24 sts)

Rows 7 to 13: 1 sc in each st, ch 1, turn.

Row 14: 1 sc in each st, ch 1, rotate the work 90 degrees clockwise and work 14 sc along the side of the vest, working in the spaces between rows. When you reach the top edge, crochet 20 sc in the remaining loops of the foundation chain. Then ch 1, rotate the piece 90 degrees clockwise again and work 14 sc along the other side of the vest, working in the spaces between rows (*see Techniques: Edging of Flat Pieces*).

Fasten off invisibly and weave in ends.

HAIR

Round 1: Using **light yellow**, 6 sc in a magic ring.

Round 2: 2 sc in each st. (12 sts)

Round 3: *1 sc, 2 sc in the next st; rep from * to end. (18 sts)

Round 4: *2 sc, 2 sc in the next st; rep from * to end. (24 sts)

Round 5: *3 sc, 2 sc in the next st; rep from * to end. (30 sts)

Round 6: *4 sc, 2 sc in the next st; rep from * to end. (36 sts)

Round 7: *5 sc, 2 sc in the next st; rep from * to end. (42 sts)

Round 8: *13 sc, 2 sc in the next st; rep from * to end. (45 sts)

Rounds 9 to 15: 1 sc in each st.

Round 16: *Ch 9, 1 sc in second ch from hook, 1 sc in each st along ch (8 sts), 2 sc, rep from * to create 22 short hair locks. Leave the last stitch of the round unworked.

Fasten off, leaving a long tail to sew to the head.

"Carry out a random act of kindness, with no expectation of reward, safe in the knowledge that one day someone might do the same for you."

TIARA

Round 1: Using **light grey**, ch 52, 1 sc in the first chain (that's the 52nd chain from hook) to form a ring (be sure not to twist the chain), 1 sc in each ch to end. (52 sts)

Rounds 2 and 3: 1 sc in each st.

Round 4: 16 slst, *(2 hdc, 1 picot st (*see Stitches: Picot Stitch*) on top of the previous st, 1 hdc) all in the same st, 3 slst, rep from * 4 more times, 16 slst.

Fasten off invisibly and weave in ends.

ASSEMBLY

Sew the hair to the head (*see Techniques: Sewing the Hair*) and part the curls on her forehead to one side.

Sew the arms to the sides of the body (*see Techniques: Sewing the Arms*).

Slip the vest onto Diana's arms. It will look like a jacket.

Place the tiara on her head.

Thread the beads with the transparent cord and create a necklace. Tie it behind Diana's neck.

Weave in all ends inside the doll.

TIP

Give a sparkly finish to the tiara by holding silver embroidery thread together with the light grey yarn to crochet the tiara.

MATERIALS

2.5mm (C/2) crochet hook

100% 8-ply cotton; colours used: skin colour, white, light grey, grey, dark grey, black, small amount of pink

Yarn needle

8mm (⅓in) safety eyes

Stitch marker

Fibrefill stuffing

FINISHED SIZE

20cm (7¾in) tall

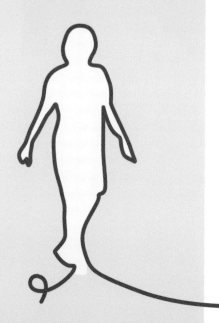

HARRIET TUBMAN

Why Harriet? Because she was one of the most courageous women in American history and an icon of freedom. She was born into slavery in Maryland but managed to escape. But she never forgot that others still lived as slaves, so she risked her life many times returning to save others. Using a network of secret roads and safe houses, known as the Underground Railroad, she rescued many people. And she was never caught. When the American Civil War began in 1861 Harriet joined the Union Army, first as a cook and nurse, then as a spy and commander. When the war was over and slavery abolished, she continued fighting to help black people find jobs and health care. Till her final days, she dedicated her life to others in need.

LEG 1

Round 1: Using **skin** colour, 6 sc in a magic ring. (6 sts)

Round 2: 2 sc in each st. (12 sts)

Rounds 3 to 8: 1 sc in each st.

Round 9: Change to **light grey** for the underwear, 1 sc BLO in each st.

Fasten off invisibly (*see Techniques: Fasten Off Invisibly*) and weave in ends (*see Techniques: Weaving In Ends*). Set aside.

LEG 2

Work as for Leg 1, but do not fasten off yarn at the end. We will continue with the body.

BODY

Round 10: Still with leg 2 on your hook, ch 3 and join to leg 1 with a sc (*see Techniques: Joining Legs*), place a stitch marker here for new beg of round, work 11 sc all along leg 1, 1 sc into each ch of 3-ch-loop, 12 sc all along leg 2 and 1 sc into other side of each ch of 3-ch-loop. (30 sts)

Round 11: *4 sc, 2 sc in the next st, rep from * to end. (36 sts)

Rounds 12 to 16: 1 sc in each st.

Stuff the legs firmly at this point.

Round 17: *4 sc, sc2tog, rep from * to end. (30 sts)

Round 18: Change to **dark grey** for the coat, 1 sc BLO in each st.

Round 19: Change back to **light grey**, 1 sc BLO in each st.

Round 20: *3 sc, sc2tog, rep from * to end. (24 sts)

Round 21: Change back to **dark grey**, 1 sc BLO in each st.

Rounds 22 and 23: 1 sc in each st.

Start to stuff the body firmly at this point and continue to stuff as you work.

Round 24: *2 sc, sc2tog, rep from * to end. (18 sts)

Rounds 25 to 27: 1 sc in each st.

Round 28: *1 sc, sc2tog, rep from * to end. (12 sts)

Round 29: 1 sc in each st.

Round 30: Change to **white** for the shirt, 1 sc BLO in each st.

Round 31: 1 sc in each st.

Do not fasten off yarn. We will continue with the head.

HEAD

Round 32: Change to **skin** colour, 1 sc BLO in each st.

Round 33: 2 sc in each st. (24 sts)

Round 34: *3 sc, 2 sc in the next st, rep from * to end. (30 sts)

Stuff the neck area firmly at this point.

Round 35: *4 sc, 2 sc in the next st, rep from * to end. (36 sts)

Round 36: *5 sc, 2 sc in the next st, rep from * to end. (42 sts)

Round 37: 1 sc in each st.

Round 38: 26 sc, 1 bobble st for the nose (*see Stitches: Bobble Stitch*), 1 sc in each st to end.

Be sure to align the nose with the middle of the legs and adjust the positioning if necessary.

We will take a break here from the head to work the collar of Harriet's coat. Place a stitch marker in the loop on your hook to secure it and cut the yarn.

COLLAR

For detailed photographs of how to work this collar *see Techniques: Making the Collars*.

Turn the body upside down and join **dark grey** in one of the front loops of round 30, at the back of the neck.

Round 1: 1 sc FLO in each st of round 30. (12 sts)

Round 2: 4 sc, (1 hdc, 1 dc) in the next st, (3 dc) in the next st, 1 slst, (1 slst, ch 2, 2 dc) in the next st, (1 dc, 1 hdc) in the next st, 3 sc. (16 sts excluding slst and ch)

Fasten off invisibly and weave in ends.

"There are two things I've got a right to, and these are, Death or Liberty — one or the other I mean to have"

We will now continue with the head. Rejoin the **skin** colour to where you stopped working the head.

Rounds 39 to 47: 1 sc in each st.

Round 48: *5 sc, sc2tog, rep from * to end. (36 sts)

Place safety eyes one round above the nose, with 8 sts between them (*see Techniques: Attaching Eyes*), embroider cheeks with **pink**.

Round 49: *4 sc, sc2tog, rep from * to end. (30 sts)

Start stuffing the head at this point.

Round 50: *3 sc, sc2tog, rep from * to end. (24 sts)

Round 51: *2 sc, sc2tog, rep from * to end. (18 sts)

Stuff firmly.

Round 52: *1 sc, sc2tog, rep from * to end. (12 sts)

Round 53: (Sc2tog) 6 times. (6 sts)

Fasten off and close the remaining stitches through the front loops (*see Techniques: Closing Remaining Stitches Through the Front Loops*). Weave in ends (*see Techniques: Hiding Ends Inside the Doll*).

SKIRT

Turn the body upside down and join **light grey** in one of the front loops of round 18, at the back of the body.

Round 1: 1 sc FLO in each st of round 18. (30 sts)

Round 2: *4 sc, 2 sc in the next st, rep from * to end. (36 sts)

Round 3: 1 sc in each st.

Round 4: *5 sc, 2 sc in the next st, rep from * to end. (42 sts)

Rounds 5 to 7: 1 sc in each st.

Round 8: *6 sc, 2 sc in the next st, rep from * to end. (48 sts)

Rounds 9 to 14: 1 sc in each st.

Round 15: *7 sc, 2 sc in the next st, rep from * to end. (54 sts)

Rounds 16 to 18: 1 sc in each st.

Fasten off invisibly and weave in ends.

COAT

Turn the body upside down and join **dark grey** in one of the front loops of round 19, at the back of the body.

Round 1: 1 sc FLO in each st of round 19. (30 sts)

Round 2: *2 sc, 2 sc in the next st, rep from * to end. (40 sts)

Round 3: 1 sc in each st.

Round 4: *7 sc, 2 sc in the next st, rep from * to end. (45 sts)

Round 5: 1 sc in each st.

Fasten off invisibly.

ARMS (MAKE TWO)

Round 1: Using **skin** colour, ch 2, 4 sc in the second ch from hook. (4 sts)

Round 2: 2 sc in each st. (8 sts)

Rounds 3 to 5: 1 sc in each st.

Round 6: Change to **dark grey** for the coat, 1 sc BLO in each st.

TIP

Harriet's skirt should touch the floor and cover her feet. To achieve this, feel free to add an extra straight round to the skirt.

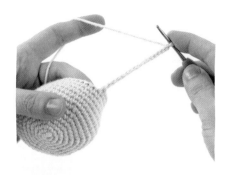

Rounds 7 to 17: 1 sc in each st.

There is no need to stuff the arms.

Round 18: Press the opening with your fingers, aligning 4 sts side by side and sc both sides together by working 1 sc into each pair of sts (*see Techniques: Closing the Arms*).

Fasten off, leaving a long tail to sew to the body.

HAIR

Round 1: Using **black**, 6 sc in a magic ring.

Round 2: 2 sc in each st. (12 sts)

Round 3: *1 sc, 2 sc in the next st; rep from * to end. (18 sts)

Round 4: *2 sc, 2 sc in the next st; rep from * to end. (24 sts)

Round 5: *3 sc, 2 sc in the next st; rep from * to end. (30 sts)

Round 6: *4 sc, 2 sc in the next st; rep from * to end. (36 sts)

Round 7: *5 sc, 2 sc in the next st; rep from * to end. (42 sts)

Round 8: *13 sc, 2 sc in the next st; rep from * to end. (45 sts)

Rounds 9 to 15: 1 sc in each st.

Round 16: 1 slst, 1 sc, 1 hdc, 10 dc, 1 hdc, 1 sc, 1 slst, 1 sc, 1 hdc, 10 dc, 1 hdc, 1 sc, 1 slst. Leave the rest of the stitches unworked.

Fasten off, leaving a long tail to sew to the head.

HEAD SCARF

Round 1: Using **light grey**, 6 sc in a magic ring.

Round 2: 2 sc in each st. (12 sts)

Round 3: *1 sc, 2 sc in the next st; rep from * to end. (18 sts)

Round 4: *2 sc, 2 sc in the next st; rep from * to end. (24 sts)

Round 5: *3 sc, 2 sc in the next st; rep from * to end. (30 sts)

Round 6: *4 sc, 2 sc in the next st; rep from * to end. (36 sts)

Round 7: *5 sc, 2 sc in the next st; rep from * to end. (42 sts)

Round 8: *6 sc, 2 sc in the next st; rep from * to end. (48 sts)

Rounds 9 to 14: 1 sc in each st.

Round 15: Ch 16 to create first strap, 1 sc in second ch from hook, 1 sc in each st along ch (15 sts), 46 sc BLO along the edge of the scarf, ch 16 for second strap, 1 sc in second ch from hook, 1 sc in each st along ch (15 sts), turn strap to join to the edge of the scarf. (76 sts)

Round 16: 46 sc FLO, 15 sc FLO along the strap. (61 sts)

Round 17: Ch 1, turn, 15 sc BLO along strap, 46 sc BLO, 15 sc BLO along second strap.

Round 18: Ch 1, turn, 15 sc BLO along second strap.

Fasten off invisibly.

SHAWL

The shawl is worked in rows, using **light grey**.

Row 1: Ch 41, 1 sc in the second ch from hook, 1 sc in each ch to end, ch 1, turn. (40 sts)

Row 2: Sc2tog, 36 sc, sc2tog, ch 1, turn. (38 sts)

Row 3: Sc2tog, 34 sc, sc2tog, ch 1, turn. (36 sts)

Row 4: Sc2tog, 32 sc, sc2tog, ch 1, turn. (34 sts)

Row 5: Sc2tog, 30 sc, sc2tog, ch 1, turn. (32 sts)

Row 6: Sc2tog, 28 sc, sc2tog, ch 1, turn. (30 sts)

Row 7: Sc2tog, 26 sc, sc2tog, ch 1, turn. (28 sts)

Row 8: Sc2tog, 24 sc, sc2tog, ch 1, turn. (26 sts)

Row 9: Sc2tog, 22 sc, sc2tog, ch 1, turn. (24 sts)

Row 10: Sc2tog, 20 sc, sc2tog, ch 1, turn. (22 sts)

Row 11: Sc2tog, 18 sc, sc2tog, ch 1, turn. (20 sts)

Row 12: Sc2tog, 16 sc, sc2tog, ch 1, turn. (18 sts)

Row 13: Sc2tog, 14 sc, sc2tog, ch 1, turn. (16 sts)

Row 14: Sc2tog, 12 sc, sc2tog, ch 1, turn. (14 sts)

Row 15: Sc2tog, 10 sc, sc2tog, ch 1, turn. (12 sts)

Row 16: Sc2tog, 8 sc, sc2tog, ch 1, turn. (10 sts)

Row 17: Sc2tog, 6 sc, sc2tog, ch 1, turn. (8 sts)

Row 18: Sc2tog, 4 sc, sc2tog, ch 1, turn. (6 sts)

Row 19: Sc2tog, 2 sc, sc2tog, ch 1, turn. (4 sts)

Row 20: (Sc2tog) twice, ch 1, turn. (2 sts)

Row 21: Sc2tog, turn, ch 1, rotate the work 90 degrees clockwise and work 21 sc along the side of the triangle, working in the spaces between rows. When you reach the top edge, crochet 40 sc in the remaining loops of the foundation chain. Then ch 1, rotate the piece 90 degrees clockwise again and work 21 sc along the other side of the triangle, working in the spaces between rows (*see Techniques: Edging of Flat Pieces*).

Fasten off invisibly and weave in ends.

ASSEMBLY

Sew the hair to the head (*see Techniques: Sewing the Hair*).

Sew the arms to the sides of the body (*see Techniques: Sewing the Arms*).

Place the head scarf onto the head and knot the straps at the back.

Cover the arms with the shawl. You can fix it in place with a pin or you can sew it with a few stitches.

Weave in all ends inside the doll.

TIP

The decreases in the shawl are traditional ones, not the invisible ones.

MATERIALS

2.5mm (C/2) crochet hook

100% 8-ply cotton;
colours used: skin colour,
white, aubergine, light
purple, dark brown, yellow,
small amount of pink

Yarn needle

8mm (⅓in) safety eyes

Stitch marker

Fibrefill stuffing

FINISHED SIZE

20cm (7¾in) tall

ADA LOVELACE

Why Ada? Because she approached mathematics and science with creativity and a never-ending desire for new discoveries. When introduced to the Analytical Engine, a mechanical general-purpose computer designed by Charles Babbage, she was bewitched. She instantly foresaw that computers could do more than maths calculations if programmed correctly. It was entirely her idea that codes could be created and fed to computers, so Ada is considered to be the first programmer. She was ahead of her time by decades, conceiving something that was only possible a century later. Her achievements, and the path she forged for others, are celebrated on Ada Lovelace Day, the second Tuesday in October.

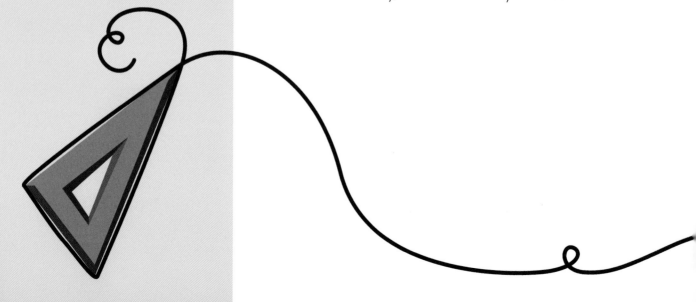

LEG 1

Round 1: Using **skin** colour, 6 sc in a magic ring. (6 sts)

Round 2: 2 sc in each st. (12 sts)

Rounds 3 to 8: 1 sc in each st.

Round 9: Change to **white** for the underwear, 1 sc BLO in each st.

Fasten off invisibly (*see Techniques: Fasten Off Invisibly*) and weave in ends (*see Techniques: Weaving In Ends*). Set aside.

LEG 2

Work as for Leg 1, but do not fasten off yarn at the end. We will continue with the body.

BODY

Round 10: Still with leg 2 on your hook, ch 3 and join to leg 1 with a sc (*see Techniques: Joining Legs*), place a stitch marker here for new beg of round, work 11 sc all along leg 1, 1 sc into each ch of 3-ch-loop, 12 sc all along leg 2 and 1 sc into other side of each ch of 3-ch-loop. (30 sts)

Round 11: *4 sc, 2 sc in the next st, rep from * to end. (36 sts)

Rounds 12 to 16: 1 sc in each st.

Stuff the legs firmly at this point.

Round 17: *4 sc, sc2tog, rep from * to end. (30 sts)

Round 18: Change to **light purple** for the dress, 1 sc in each st.

Round 19: Change to **aubergine** for the belt, 1 sc BLO in each st.

Round 20: *3 sc, sc2tog, rep from * to end. (24 sts)

Round 21: Change back to **light purple** for the dress, 1 sc in each st.

Rounds 22 and 23: 1 sc in each st.

Start to stuff the body firmly at this point and continue to stuff as you work.

Round 24: *2 sc, sc2tog, rep from * to end. (18 sts)

Rounds 25 and 26: 1 sc in each st.

Round 27: *1 sc, sc2tog, rep from * to end. (12 sts)

Now we will do several colour changes. Remember to join the yarn of the required colour in the last step of the previous st to the change.

Round 28: 7 sc, change to **white**, 1 sc, change back to **light purple**, 4 sc.

Round 29: 6 sc, change to **white**, 3 sc, change back to **light purple**, 3 sc.

Round 30: 5 sc, change to **white**, 5 sc, change back to **light purple**, 2 sc.

Round 31: 4 sc, change to **white**, 7 sc, change back to **light purple**, 1 sc.

You should have a white triangle at the front centre of the doll.

Do not fasten off yarn. We will continue with the head.

"The more I study, the more insatiable do I feel my genius for it to be."

HEAD

Round 32: Change to **skin** colour, 1 sc BLO in each of the first 4 sts (those in **light purple**), 1 sc BLO in each of the following 7 sts (those in **white**), 1 sc BLO in the last st (in **light purple**). (12 sts)

Round 33: 2 sc in each st. (24 sts)

Round 34: *3 sc, 2 sc in the next st, rep from * to end. (30 sts)
Stuff the neck area firmly at this point.

Round 35: *4 sc, 2 sc in the next st, rep from * to end. (36 sts)

Round 36: *5 sc, 2 sc in the next st, rep from * to end. (42 sts)

Round 37: 1 sc in each st.

Round 38: 29 sc, 1 bobble st for the nose (*see Stitches: Bobble Stitch*), 1 sc in each st to end.

Be sure to align the nose with the middle of the legs, and the white triangle at the neck, and adjust the positioning if necessary.

Rounds 39 to 47: 1 sc in each st.

Round 48: *5 sc, sc2tog, rep from * to end. (36 sts)
Place safety eyes one round above the nose, with 8 sts between them (*see Techniques: Attaching Eyes*), embroider cheeks with **pink**.

Round 49: *4 sc, sc2tog, rep from * to end. (30 sts)
Start stuffing the head at this point.

Round 50: *3 sc, sc2tog, rep from * to end. (24 sts)

Round 51: *2 sc, sc2tog, rep from * to end. (18 sts)
Stuff firmly.

Round 52: *1 sc, sc2tog, rep from * to end. (12 sts)

Round 53: (Sc2tog) 6 times. (6 sts)

Fasten off and close the remaining stitches through the front loops (*see Techniques: Closing Remaining Stitches Through the Front Loops*). Weave in ends (*see Techniques: Hiding Ends Inside the Doll*).

SKIRT

Turn the body upside down and join **light purple** in one of the front loops of round 19, at the back of the body.

Round 1: 1 sc FLO in each st of round 19. (30 sts)

Round 2: *4 sc, 2 sc in the next st, rep from * to end. (36 sts)

Round 3: 1 sc in each st.

Round 4: *5 sc, 2 sc in the next st, rep from * to end. (42 sts)

Rounds 5 to 7: 1 sc in each st.

Round 8: *6 sc, 2 sc in the next st, rep from * to end. (48 sts)

Rounds 9 to 14: 1 sc in each st.

Round 15: *7 sc, 2 sc in the next st, rep from * to end. (54 sts)

Rounds 16 to 18: 1 sc in each st.

Round 19: Change to **aubergine**, 1 sc in each st.

Fasten off invisibly and weave in ends.

TIP

There's no right or wrong when making Ada's hairbun. Just twist the locks and secure the resulting shape with some stitches.

ARMS (MAKE TWO)

Round 1: Using **skin** colour, ch 2, 4 sc in the second ch from hook. (4 sts)

Round 2: 2 sc in each st. (8 sts)

Rounds 3 to 5: 1 sc in each st.

Round 6: Change to **aubergine**, 1 sc BLO in each st.

Round 7: 1 sc in each st.

Round 8: Change to **light purple**, 1 sc in each st.

Rounds 9 to 16: 1 sc in each st.

Round 17: Press the opening with your fingers, aligning 4 sts side by side and sc both sides together by working 1 sc into each pair of sts (*see Techniques: Closing the Arms*).

Fasten off, leaving a long tail to sew to the body.

COLLAR

Row 1: Using **aubergine** and leaving a long initial tail, ch 25. Starting from the second ch from hook, 3 slst, 3 sc, 3 hdc, 6 dc, 3 hdc, 3 sc, 3 slst. (24 sts)

Fasten off, leaving a long tail to sew to the neck.

HAIR

Round 1: Using **dark brown**, 6 sc in a magic ring.

Round 2: 2 sc in each st. (12 sts)

Round 3: *1 sc, 2 sc in the next st; rep from * to end. (18 sts)

Round 4: *2 sc, 2 sc in the next st; rep from * to end. (24 sts)

Round 5: *3 sc, 2 sc in the next st; rep from * to end. (30 sts)

Round 6: *4 sc, 2 sc in the next st; rep from * to end. (36 sts)

Round 7: *5 sc, 2 sc in the next st; rep from * to end. (42 sts)

Round 8: *13 sc, 2 sc in the next st; rep from * to end. (45 sts)

Rounds 9 to 15: 1 sc in each st.

Round 16: 1 slst, *ch 101, 1 sc in second ch from hook, 1 sc in each st along ch (100 sts), 1 slst; rep from * once more. Leave the rest of the stitches of the round unworked.

Fasten off, leaving a long tail to sew to the head.

HEADBAND

Row 1: Using **yellow** and leaving a long initial tail, ch 36.

Fasten off, leaving a long tail to sew to the head.

BIG ROSETTE

Round 1: Using **yellow**, 6 sc in a magic ring.

Round 2: 2 sc in each st. (12 sts)

Round 3: *1 slst, (1 sc, 1 hdc, 1 sc) in the next st; rep from * 5 more times, 1 slst in first st of round to finish.

Fasten off, leaving a long tail to sew to the headband.

SMALL ROSETTE

Round 1: Using **yellow**, 8 sc in a magic ring.

Round 2: *1 slst, (1 sc, 1 hdc, 1 sc) in the next st; rep from * 3 more times, 1 slst in first st of round to finish.

Fasten off, leaving a long tail to sew to the headband.

ASSEMBLY

Using **aubergine** and the yarn needle, embroider small straight lines to the skirt of the dress.

Sew the collar around the white triangle on Ada's neck, joining the ends first then around the neck with a few stitches.

Sew the arms to the sides of the body (*see Techniques: Sewing the Arms*).

Sew the hair onto the head (*see Techniques: Sewing the Hair*), with the two super long hair locks over the forehead. Do not sew them yet.

Sew the headband to the head, first from one side then to the other.

Now part the two long locks and fix them with a stitch or two over each end of the headband.

Then secure the locks in the upper back of the hair and twist them together to create a loose bun. Secure the shape in place with a few stitches.

Sew the big rosette to one side of the headband and then sew the smaller rosette on top of the bigger one.

Weave in all ends inside the doll.

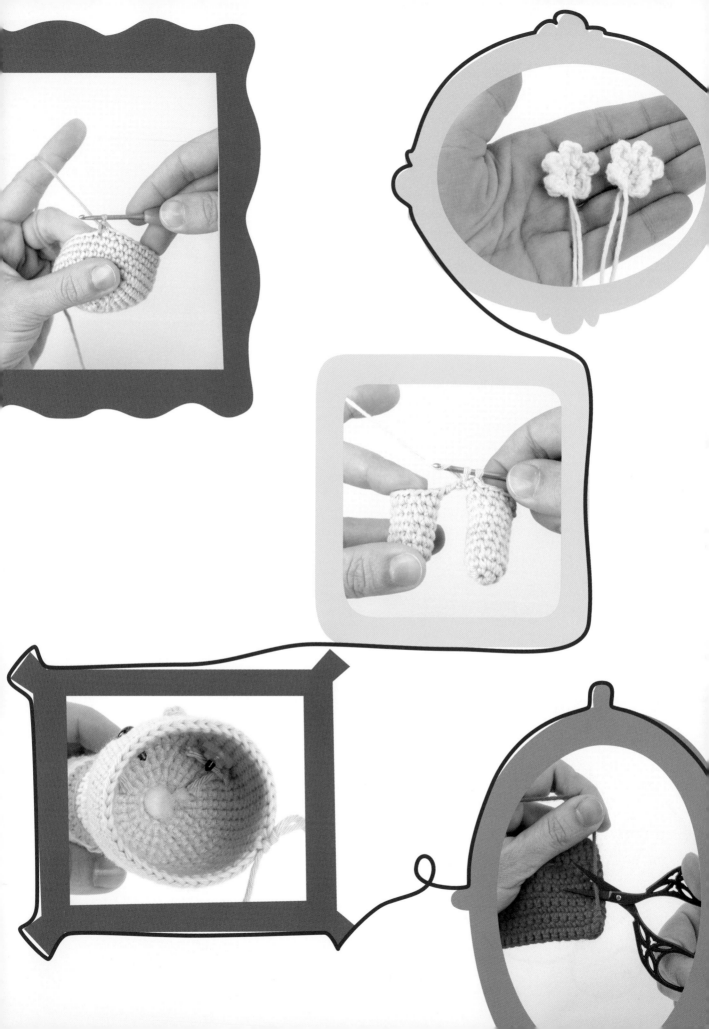

TECHNIQUES

Here you will find all of the techniques that you need to create your
dolls and their accessories. I have included an explanation for each
technique, along with lots of photos, so that you can follow them
easily. You may prefer to use your own methods, and that's fine too,
but they're here if you need them and I hope they help you with the
placement of your hook or stitches and to sew your dolls together.

TIP

An invisible single crochet decrease is used to make your decreasing less visible by working into the front loops only of the stitches.

ANATOMY OF A STITCH

Every finished stitch looks like a sideways letter **v**, with two loops meeting at one end (**1**). The loop closer to you is the **front loop** and the loop behind it is the **back loop**. You will sometimes be asked to crochet certain stitches in the front loops (FLO) or in the back loops (BLO) only and there's always a reason for this: you will use the remaining loops later!

INCREASING

This means working two stitches in the same stitch (**2**). After you have worked the first stitch, you simply insert your hook back into the same place and work the next stitch.

INVISIBLE SINGLE CROCHET DECREASE

An invisible crochet decrease means working two stitches together at the same time, so that it isn't noticeable. Insert the hook in the front loop of the next stitch (**3**) and in the front loop of the stitch next to that, one at a time (**4**). Yarn over hook and draw it through both front loops in one go. Yarn over hook again and draw it through the two remaining loops on your hook (**5**). The invisible single crochet decrease only works for three-dimensional pieces that will be stuffed later.

REGULAR SINGLE CROCHET DECREASE

To crochet the shawl used by Harriet Tubman, which is a flat piece, you should use a regular single crochet decrease which is worked just the same as an invisible single crochet decrease, but you insert your hook under both loops of the stitches.

CHANGING COLOUR

To change to another colour you should join the new colour during the final step of the last stitch in the previous colour. This means that when the last two loops of the stitch remain on your hook (**1**), you should grab the new colour, wrap it around your hook (**2**) and pull it through those two loops. This will leave the new colour on your hook (**3**), ready to work the next stitch in that colour (**4**).

When working pieces that will be stuffed later, I cut the yarn of the old colour and tie this into a knot with the new colour, inside of the piece, to secure both tails. This can only be done in three-dimensional pieces, of course, because these knots will remain inside the doll and won't be visible. When working flat pieces that have a right and wrong side, you will have to weave in the ends in between the stitches on the wrong side.

FASTEN OFF INVISIBLY

This method avoids the little stub that can look unsightly when you fasten off your crochet. When you have your final loop on the hook and have finished your crochet, cut the yarn, take the yarn over the hook and pull all the way through the final loop. Pull the yarn tight, which creates a small knot. Thread the yarn tail onto a tapestry needle and insert the needle, from the back of the work, underneath the top **v** of the second stitch along the main edge (**5**). Pull the yarn all the way through. Insert the needle from the front, into the top **v** of the last stitch made and pull the yarn through (**6**). You have created a 'mimic' stitch that covers the small knot and joins up the round neatly.

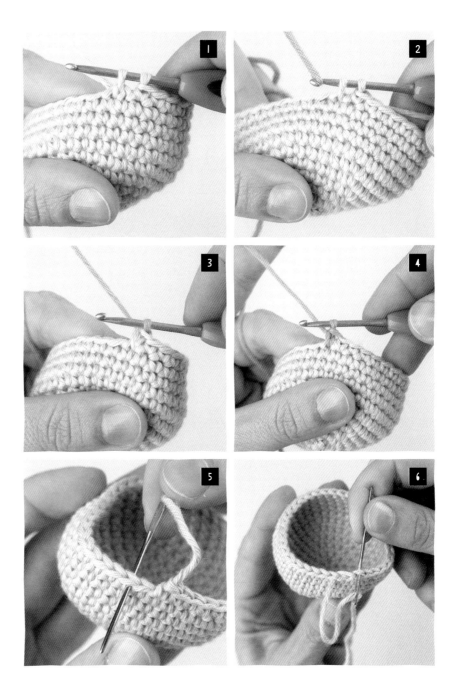

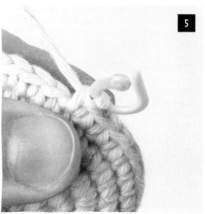

TIP

You can use proper stitch markers to mark your first stitch of the round, or you can use paper clips, hair clips or even little pieces of yarn!

CLOSING REMAINING STITCHES THROUGH THE FRONT LOOPS

After the final round, you may be instructed to close the remaining stitches through the front loops. To do this, fasten off after the last stitch and thread the yarn onto a tapestry needle. Insert the needle through each visible loop of the last round of stitches (through one loop of the stitch only) (**1**). When you reach the end, pull gently to close up the gap (**2**). Secure the thread with a few stitches and hide the ends inside the doll.

HIDING ENDS INSIDE THE DOLL

Insert your crochet hook into the doll, between stitches, a few centimetres (a couple of inches) from the tail end that you want to hide, then push the hook out between stitches that are close to the tail end, making sure that the hook is really close to the tail end of yarn (**3**). Take yarn over hook and pull through the doll and as you pull out your hook, the yarn will come with it. Snip the yarn close to the doll to leave a clean finish (**4**).

WORKING IN ROWS

Flat pieces are worked in rows, starting with a foundation chain. This is a string of chain stitches. It's important not to twist the chain, so keep a tight grip on the crocheted chains near your hook.

WORKING IN ROUNDS

All the dolls in this book have the same body structure and they are worked in rounds, in a continuous spiral, so there's no need to close the round after finishing each one. That is why the use of a stitch marker is important to mark the beginning of each round (**5**). Move this stitch marker up as you work.

MAGIC RING

Round pieces always start with a magic ring because, when tightened, it will leave no holes in the middle where stuffing could come out. To make a magic ring, start in the same way that you would a slip knot, by making a loop shape with the tail end of the yarn. Insert the hook into it and draw another loop of yarn through it, but do not pull the tail end. As well as the loop on your hook, you will have a large loop sitting beneath your hook, with a twisted section of yarn (**1**). It is important that you work into the centre of the loop for your first round, and also that you work over the twisted section of yarn (**2**). When you have completed your first round, you can pull the yarn tail tight to close the hole (**3**).

JOINING LEGS

You will always start the dolls in this book by crocheting the legs, which need to be joined, then continue with the body up to the head.

You will crochet one leg first and set it aside while you crochet the second leg. Then, with leg 2 still on your hook, you will chain 3 to join leg 1 with a sc (**4**). This will be the new beginning of the following rounds, so it's important to place a stitch marker there. You will then have to crochet a further 11 sc all along leg 1 and, after that, crochet 3 sc in one of the sides of the 3-ch-loop (**5**). Then, crochet 12 sc along leg 2 (**6**) so you can finally work 3 sc on the other side of the 3-ch-loop (**7**). You will end up with a round of 30 stitches which will be the beginning of the body of your doll.

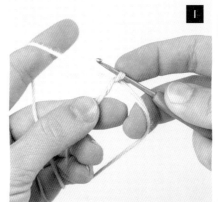
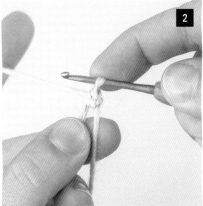
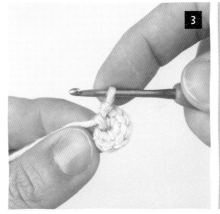

TIP

You may need to practise a magic ring a few times before you feel totally comfortable with the technique, but if you can persevere and master it, the start of your crochet will be really neat.

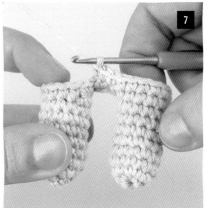

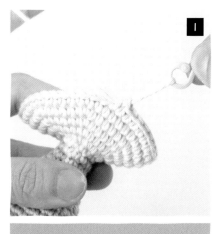

TIP

For extra security when attaching the safety eyes, add some craft glue to the washer or melt the rod slightly with a lighter.

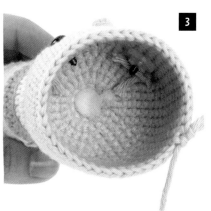

INTERRUPTING YOUR WORK

Sometimes I will recommend you to stop crocheting the head at some point before finishing to crochet a collar without having the stuffed head interfering with the movement of your hands. To do this, you can place a stitch marker on the loop on your hook, so the stitches won't come off (**1**). Then you can cut the yarn (**2**). When you are ready, you can join the yarn again as you would do for a colour change.

ATTACHING EYES

Safety eyes have two parts: the front with a straight or threaded rod, and a washer that goes inside the toy. If fastened correctly, it's almost impossible to remove them (**3**). But beware, if you are crocheting the doll for a small child, you should probably consider embroidering them with **black** or **dark brown** leftover pieces of yarn.

SEWING THE CHEEKS

These are made whilst the head is in progress, after you have attached the safety eyes (if using). Use a short length of **pink** yarn and thread onto a tapestry needle. Working from the inside of the head, in line with lower edge of the eye and a few stitches away, make a small straight running stitch over one or two stitches, bringing the needle back through to inside of head. Repeat this two or three times to make the cheek thicker. Tie off the ends (**4** and **5**).

MAKING THE COLLARS

Join the required yarn in the middle of the back of the neck of your doll and crochet: 1 sc FLO in each st of the round. Then, in round 2, crochet 4 sc, (1 hdc, 1 dc) in the next st, (3 dc) in the next st (**1**), 1 slst, (1 slst, ch 2 (**2**), 2 dc) in the next st, (1 dc, 1 hdc) in the next st, 3 sc. (16 sts excluding slst and ch). Fasten off and weave in ends (**3**).

WEAVING IN ENDS

With the wrong side of your piece facing, thread the tail end onto a tapestry needle and insert the needle underneath the posts of three or four stitches (**4**). Pull the yarn through and snip close to the work (**5**). If you feel it necessary you can repeat this process by working back through the same stitches: skip the first stitch and then insert your needle underneath the next few stitches. Pull the yarn through and snip it off close to the work.

TIP

The slst should sit right below the nose. If it does not, unravel and add or substract the necessary sc in the beginning of round 2 to adjust the positioning.

JOINING THE YARN TO BEGIN A SKIRT OR COLLAR

Some details that build the wardrobe of these characters, like skirts, are crocheted to the body of the doll and are not removable. To this end you will always find that the pattern calls for a special round where you will work into the back loop only in the body of your doll, then to add the skirt or collar you will work into the remaining front loops.

To join in the yarn to create a skirt, dress, coat or collar, you will always need to hold your doll's head down (even if the head is not quite finished) and look for the remaining front loop right in the middle of the back of your doll. I usually pick the last front loop of the round (which is next to the first front loop of the round) and join my yarn right there and then crochet towards the left (**1**).

CLOSING THE ARMS

The arms of the dolls look like crochet tubes and they do not need to be filled with stuffing. In the last round you will be asked to close the tube by flattening the opening, so that 4 stitches of the top layer become aligned with 4 stitches of the lower layer (**2**). Once you've achieved this, join both layers by crocheting 1 sc in each pair of stitches (**3**). You will end up with 4 sc (**4**). Fasten off but remember to leave a long yarn tail to sew to the body (**5**).

CREATING ARMHOLES ON VESTS

Armholes are created over two rows and full instructions are included for each doll's vest. On the first row, you make a chain of stitches (**6**) then skip as many stitches as indicated before working the next sc (**7**). This creates a chain loop which is the gap for the armhole. On the next row, you work stitches into the chain loops (**8**) and the armholes are complete.

EDGING OF FLAT PIECES

Many of the flat pieces have a crocheted edge to create a neat finish. To do this, you will work as many stitches as instructed in the pattern, working either along the edge and inserting your hook in between the spaces between rows (**1**), or into stitches themselves (**2**), depending on which edge you are working along.

SEWING THE ARMS

Thread the yarn tail onto a tapestry needle and place the arm against the side of the body. When you are happy with the placement insert the needle through a stitch on the body (**3**) and pull the yarn through. Insert the needle through the top of the next stitch on the arm (**4**) and pull the yarn through. Repeat this process until the arm is sewn in place (**5**). Secure the yarn with a few stitches and follow the instructions for hiding the ends inside the doll.

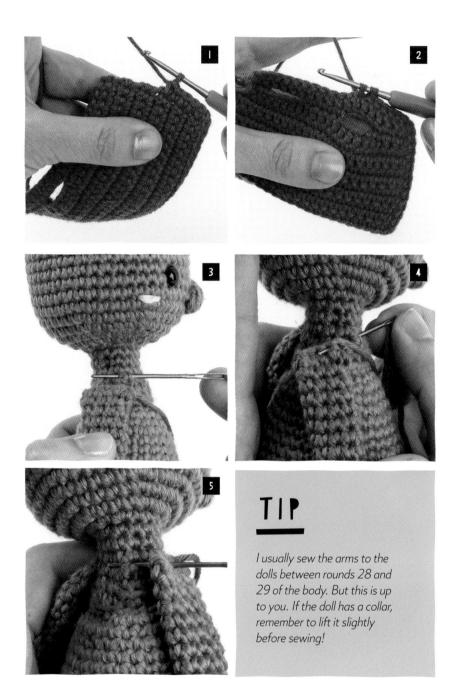

TIP

I usually sew the arms to the dolls between rounds 28 and 29 of the body. But this is up to you. If the doll has a collar, remember to lift it slightly before sewing!

TIP

The hair locks will tend to curl naturally as you go, but if they don't, you can help them with your fingers, by twisting them into shape like a corkscrew.

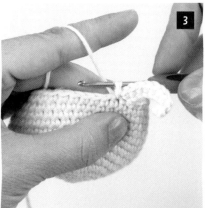

CROCHETING CURLS

Many of the dolls in this book have curls; some of them are short, like those on Diana, Princess of Wales or Grace Hopper, and some of them are longer like those on Dolly Parton. All these curls start with a foundation chain (the length of which will be indicated in the pattern), working from the hair cap (**1**), then you will crochet 1 sc in the back loop of each chain stitch (**2**) until you reach the edge of the hair piece again (**3**). Do not use the back bumps of the foundation chain unless specified. These hair locks will tend to curl naturally as you go, but if they don't, help them with your fingers, twisting them into shape.

SEWING THE HAIR

Use small straight stitches to sew the hair to the head, working over the sc stitches of the hair (**4**) and making sure that you also work through the stitches of the head, to join them securely. It's OK to space the stitches out as you don't need to work over every stitch (**5**). Don't pull the yarn too tightly when sewing, otherwise your stitches may distort the shape of the head. Use matching coloured yarn so that these stitches are not visible.

SEWING LOOSE PIECES

If required, stuff the piece to be sewn. Thread the tapestry needle and position the piece in place. Secure it with pins. Do you like it there? Then let's go! Using backstitching, sew the piece with your needle going under both loops of the last round.

FLOWERS

First you will work the first round of 5 dc into a magic ring as instructed in the pattern.

Work 1 slst in the next stitch, ch 2 (**1**).

Yarn over hook, insert the hook back into the same stitch, yarn over hook and pull yarn through the st (**2**).

Yarn over hook, pull yarn through two loops on your hook (**3**).

Yarn over hook, insert hook into the same stitch, yarn over hook and pull yarn through the stitch (**4**).

Yarn over hook, pull yarn through the first two loops on your hook (**5**).

Yarn over hook, pull yarn through the three remaining loops on your hook, ch 2 (**6**).

Work 1 slst in the same st (**7**).

Repeat steps 1 to 7 a further 4 times to make 5 petals; finish with a slst in the next st. Make as many flowers as instructed (**8**).

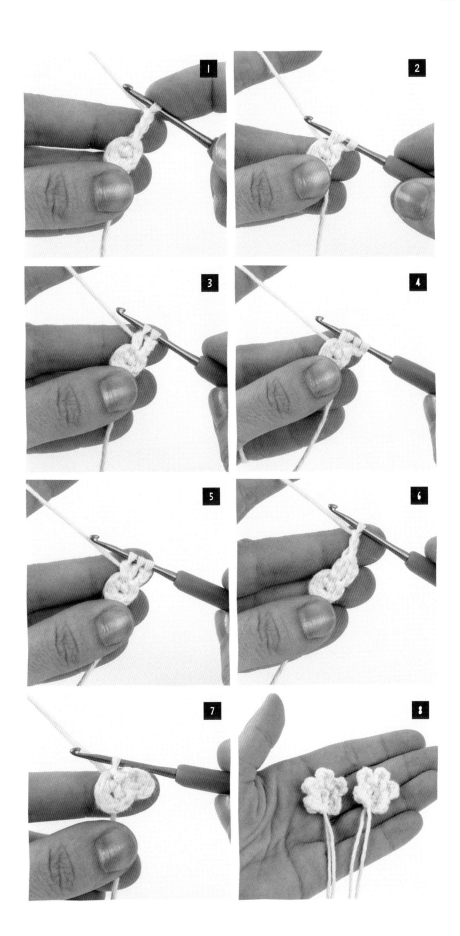

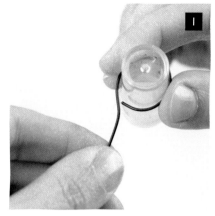

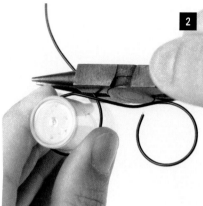

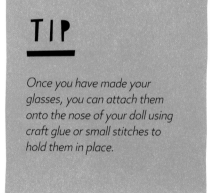

TIP

Once you have made your glasses, you can attach them onto the nose of your doll using craft glue or small stitches to hold them in place.

MAKING GLASSES

Grace Hopper wears glasses and here is the best way to make them.

First, take a small plastic lid or tube, approximately 1cm (³⁄₈in) in diameter. Wrap your wire around the lid fully, to create the first lens, and then bend the wire away slightly where it meets to start forming the bridge for the nose (**1**).

Leave approximately 1cm (³⁄₈in) of straight wire for the bridge and then wrap the wire around the plastic lid or tube again, to create the second lens (**2**).

Snip the wire where the second lens meets (**3**).

Use the pliers to close up the gaps as much as possible where the wires meet and to complete your glasses (**4** and **5**).

SOME ADDITIONAL NOTES

The bodies of these dolls, and most of their hair features and accessories, are crocheted by working in a spiral. Remember to mark the beginning of each round with a stitch marker. No need to close each round with a slip stitch.

When changing colours, you'll get a 'step' in the fabric and yes, we all hate it. There is no way to avoid it, so embrace it and try to place it at the back of your dolls!

I usually use bits of **pink** yarn to embroider the cheeks of the dolls. But you can also opt for fabric blushes or markers!

Can I wash these dolls? Yes, you can! If you only want to remove a small stain, just dampen the area with a wet cloth and a bit of soap. If you want to wash the doll completely, place it in the washing machine: gentle cycle and tumble dry low. Warning: some colours might fade just a bit.

MAKE YOUR OWN ICON

I hope that I've now inspired you to get creative and make your own crocheted icon. You can mix and match outfits, make hair curls longer or shorter, and change the colours or skin tones to create your own special icons.

ABOUT THE AUTHOR

Hello! Here we meet again! I'm Carla and, as you know, I physically live in Buenos Aires, Argentina. I say physically, because my mind and spirit are always wandering, lost in a world of yarns and colours, constantly trying to create new dolls. My hook is my magic wand! Whatever I must do during the day (work, laundry, cooking), I do while mentally thinking up new doll clothes, hairstyles and body shapes. This is why many of my creations are born as drawings on napkins, paper towels, bills or little pieces of paper I find around the house.

This book you are holding is my third book of crochet patterns with my dear friends at David and Charles and I must pinch myself. What if I wake up? I still find it hard to believe that the dolls I design get to go to all the corners of the planet because you make them come to life when following my patterns. This is the definition of a dream come true to me. I hope this book makes you as happy as it has made me while writing it for you. I'll be waiting to see the many adventures of your makes!

ACKNOWLEDGEMENTS

Thank you so much my dear friends and followers for supporting me once again! I have received such an overwhelming positive feedback to *Crochet Iconic Women*, that I am truly happy to dedicate this new book to you all.

Sarah Callard, thank you so much for leading this team! It is such a pleasure to work with you! I must thank God and the universe for sending you my way!

Can I please ask for a standing ovation to Lucy Ridley for her incredible design and to Jason Jenkins for his amazing photos? We make such a great team, guys! From my early train to Exeter, to the last quick photos late in the afternoon, I enjoy every minute of working with you.

This book wouldn't be possible without the technical editing of Carol Ibbetson and Marie Clayton and the thorough overseeing of Jess Cropper! I think these ladies have some special power, or drink a certain magic potion for breakfast, because they were able to detect all my typos and mistakes. Thank you so much!!

I am also very grateful to the amazing Sophie Seager for her wonderful ideas to promote my work and the entire team at David and Charles for receiving me every time with such welcoming smiles and hugs!

Once again, I could not have done this without the love and support (and extreme patience) of my dear family, especially my husband and my children, Iñaki and Homero. Much of the time I dedicate to crochet I take away from them. Thank you for understanding. I hope seeing so many Iconic Women around the house inspires my boys to become honest, respectful and committed men in the future.

INDEX

As the publisher, we want to honour the struggles experienced by many of the women featured in this collection by supporting a charity that works to empower girls through education.

We are happy to announce that 5% of the receipts from this book will be donated to WONDER foundation, a woman-led non-profit organization dedicated to transforming the lives of women, girls and their communities through access to quality education.

WONDER was established as a charity in 2012 as the Women's Network for Development and Educational Resources (WONDER), with a drive to empowering vulnerable people through education.

Their Vision

WONDER is working towards a future where women and girls are empowered to make informed life choices and lead the way in their own personal development.

Their Mission

To empower women, girls and their community through access to quality education so that they can exit poverty for good.

Find out more at **www.wonderfoundation.org.uk**

Printed in Turkey by Omur for:
David and Charles, Ltd
Suite A, Tourism House, Pynes Hill, Exeter, EX2 5WS

10 9 8 7 6 5 4 3 2 1

Publishing Director: Ame Verso
Senior Commissioning Editor: Sarah Callard
Managing Editor: Jeni Chown
Editor: Jessica Cropper
Project Editors: Carol Ibbetson and Marie Clayton
Head of Design: Anna Wade
Designer and Illustrator: Lucy Ridley
Photographer: Jason Jenkins
Pre-Press Designer: Ali Stark
Production Manager: Beverley Richardson

David and Charles publishes high-quality books on a wide range of subjects. For more information visit www.davidandcharles.com.

Share your makes with us on social media using #dandcbooks and follow us on Facebook and Instagram by searching for @dandcbooks.

Layout of the digital edition of this book may vary depending on reader hardware and display settings.